A Carer's Guide to

Greg Wilkinson

Tony Kendrick

Bruce Moore

SECOND EDITION

The ROYAL
SOCIETY *of*
MEDICINE
PRESS *Limited*

PUBLISHED WITH AN EDUCATIONAL GRANT FROM ELI LILLY AND COMPANY LIMITED

1 Wimpole Street, London W1M 8AE, UK

207 E Westminster Road, Lake Forest, IL 60045, USA

http://www.roysocmed.ac.uk

British Library Cataloguing in Publication Data

A catalogue record for this book is available from the British Library

First published 1996
Second edition 2000
Reprinted 2001

ISBN 1-85315-408-3

Composition by Ken Brooks, Sawbridgeworth, Herts, UK

Printed in Great Britain by Ebenezer Baylis, The Trinity Press, Worcester

Contents

Chapter 1   What is schizophrenia?   1

Chapter 2   What causes schizophrenia?   8

Chapter 3   Medical treatment   16

Chapter 4   The family, community and other treatments   24

Chapter 5   Getting help   30

Chapter 6   Mental Health Act legislation   42

Chapter 7   Problems associated with schizophrenia   55

Chapter 8   Helping carers   63

Appendix   Some commonly used words and phrases explained   69

The Authors

PROFESSOR GREG WILKINSON graduated in Medicine at Edinburgh University and trained as a psychiatrist at the Maudsley Hospital in London. He is Professor of Liaison Psychiatry at the University of Liverpool where he has responsibility for patient care, teaching medical students and undertaking research on mental health problems. Professor Wilkinson is editor of the *British Journal of Psychiatry*.

PROFESSOR TONY KENDRICK has been a GP for 14 years. He is Professor of Primary Medical Care at the University of Southampton. He still practises in a local surgery, as well as teaching medical students and researching mental health problems in general practice.

DR BRUCE MOORE graduated in medicine at Liverpool University in 1993. He has trained in general psychiatry in Liverpool and in neuropsychiatry at The National Hospital for Neurology in London. He is currently involved in full-time research into severe mental illness, and teaches psychiatry to medical undergraduates and psychiatry trainees.

Acknowledgement

Mr Mike Davis, Mental Health Act Administrator, has been a rich and ready mine of information on issues of law and we would like to thank him for his helpful comments and guidance on mental health legislation.

I What is schizophrenia?

Schizophrenia is a broad term used to describe a serious mental illness that affects the way people think and experience things. For example, a person suffering from schizophrenia may hear voices, which seem to come from nowhere and say strange things, and this may cause the sufferer to believe that they are being watched. This is usually very frightening and may lead to bizarre behaviour, such as avoiding people or relating to friends and family in a strange manner. But schizophrenia

affects different people in different ways: some sufferers are mainly withdrawn; some are quite suspicious; some seem to see or hear people who may not exist; and some appear to behave in a silly or childish manner. Many patients show a combination of these features, which may occur at different times during the course of their illness.

Schizophrenia is one of the most severe of the psychiatric disorders and, despite modern treatment methods and rehabilitation, it remains a major source of personal distress and social difficulties. The stigma surrounding schizophrenia persists, such that it is often wrongly thought of as being frequently associated with violence. In reality, most people with schizophrenia are not violent; if there is any aggression, they often direct it towards themselves in the form of self-harm or even suicide.

Who gets schizophrenia?

Schizophrenia is found in all cultures and affects one in 100 people at some time in their life. At any one time, between three and four in every 1000 people experience problems associated with schizophrenia. The disease usually begins in adolescence or early adult life, and affects both sexes equally — although it tends to occur earlier in men by about five years. The earlier the illness begins, the worse the long-term consequences for leading a normal life tend to be.

After a first episode of schizophrenia, there is a tendency for the illness to recur and for some degree of long-term disability to develop. A quarter of sufferers recover within five years; two-thirds show a fluctuating course over tens of years; and one in 10 develops an incapacitating, long-term illness.

Symptoms of schizophrenia

There is no laboratory test for schizophrenia and the diagnosis is based on the patient's symptoms. Symptoms are divided into frightening positive symptoms on the one hand, such as hallucinations (false sensations) and delusions (false beliefs), and negative symptoms on the other, such as blunted emotions, a lack of interest and energy, apathy and social withdrawal. There are also distortions of thought processes and perception, and inappropriate moods. No single symptom clinches the diagnosis, but those that often occur together include:

A   Disturbances of thinking: eg, complaints of thoughts being inserted or withdrawn from the mind and of hearing thoughts broadcast aloud.

B   Delusions of being controlled (by electricity or unspecified powers).

C   Hallucinatory voices giving a running commentary on the patient's behaviour or discussing the patient among them, or coming from some part of the patient's body.

D   Persistent delusions of other kinds that are inappropriate and/or impossible, such as having a religious or political identity (imagining that they are God or the President), or superhuman powers and abilities.

E   Persistent hallucinations accompanied by delusions when occurring for weeks or months on end.

F   Breaks in train of thought, resulting in incoherent or irrelevant speech, or the use of made-up new words.

G   Catatonic behaviour such as excitement, strange posturing, becoming mute or seeming in a stupor.

H   Negative symptoms such as apathy, poor speech and emotional responses, social withdrawal, and lowered social performance.

I   Significant and consistent change in personal behaviour, shown as a loss of interest, aimlessness, idleness, or a self-absorbed attitude and social withdrawal

Adapted from ICD-10

People with schizophrenia may also suffer from symptoms of anxiety, depression and other milder symptoms of emotional distress. An important aspect of schizophrenia is the social disablement which occurs, with work and social skills impaired, and difficulties in personal relationships. These problems can be made worse by the response of other people to them — particularly when symptoms cause social comment or disapproval.

Diagnosis of schizophrenia

Over a period of weeks or months before the onset of schizophrenia, the sufferer may lose interest in work, social activities, personal appearance and hygiene, experience anxiety and depression and become preoccupied. This is called the prodromal phase. The medical approach to diagnosis depends on the patient's symptoms falling into various categories. The International Classification of Diseases System (ICD-10, 1992) normally requires the presence of at least one very clear symptom (and usually two or more, if the first is less clear-cut) from groups A to D (above), or that symptoms from at least two of groups E to H have been present for most of the time for at least one month.

The diagnosis of schizophrenia should not be made in the presence of severe depression or manic symptoms, unless the schizophrenic illness pre-dated a mood disturbance. If schizophrenic and mood symptoms develop together and are evenly balanced, a diagnosis of schizo-affective disorder is sometimes made. Schizophrenia should not be diagnosed where there is an obvious brain disease or during drug intoxication or withdrawal of alcohol or drugs. The main American diagnostic criteria (DSM-IV, 1994) for the diagnosis of schizophrenia are fairly precise and are shown below for comparison with the ICD-10.

A Characteristic symptoms

- Two (or more) of the following are noticeable for a significant portion of time during a one-month period (or less, if successfully treated):
(1) Delusions
(2) Hallucinations
(3) Disorganized speech
(4) Grossly disorganized or catatonic behaviour
(5) Negative symptoms

B Social/occupational dysfunction

- For a large portion of the time since the start of the disturbance, one or more major areas of life such as work, interpersonal relations, or self-care, decline. When the onset is in childhood or adolescence, patients may not reach expected levels of interpersonal, educational or occupational achievement

C Duration

- Continuous signs of the disturbance persist for at least six months. This six-month period must include at least one month of symptoms (or less if successfully treated) that meet Criterion A and may include periods of prodromal or residual symptoms. During these prodromal or residual periods, the signs of the disturbance may be negative symptoms only, or else mild forms of two or more of the symptoms listed in Criterion A. Diagnosis must rule out the possibility of the condition being due to the direct physiological effects of drugs (abuse or a medication), or a general medical condition

Adapted from DSM-IV

Course of the illness

There are four basic patterns of schizophrenic illness:

(1) A single episode of illness with complete recovery.

(2) Bouts of illness with acute symptoms, few negative symptoms, often with obvious causes, and followed by a good recovery.

(3) Chronic illness with negative symptoms and disturbance of thought processes, but few signs of acute illness, no obvious causes, and social isolation, withdrawal and odd behaviour. The outlook for this pattern is usually poor.

(4) A combination of acute illness and gradually increasing chronic difficulties

These patterns of illness are illustrated in the diagram below.

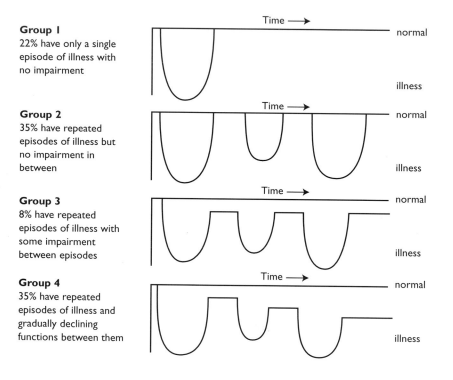

Group 1
22% have only a single episode of illness with no impairment

Group 2
35% have repeated episodes of illness but no impairment in between

Group 3
8% have repeated episodes of illness with some impairment between episodes

Group 4
35% have repeated episodes of illness and gradually declining functions between them

Patterns of schizophrenic illness (from Frangou and Murray, 1997)

Types of schizophrenia

PARANOID SCHIZOPHRENIA

This is the most common form of schizophrenic illness in which the patient usually suffers from stable delusions, often hearing voices (auditory hallucinations) alongside them. Onset tends to be later than in other forms of schizophrenia and the course tends to be either continuous or in bouts with partial or complete recovery inbetween them. In the chronic form, symptoms persist over many years.

Paranoid delusions include:

- Feelings of being persecuted, being referred to in the news, being of royal birth, being on a special mission to save mankind, having bodily changes, or of unaccountable jealousy.
- Hallucinatory voices may threaten the patient or give commands; or sounds such as whistling, humming, or laughing may be heard.
- Hallucinations of smell or taste or vision, or of sexual or other bodily sensations, sometimes occur.

——— HEBEPHRENIC SCHIZOPHRENIA

This form of schizophrenia usually starts with negative symptoms experienced between the ages of 15 and 25 years and tends to have a poor prognosis. Mood changes are marked, delusions and hallucinations are less obvious and behaviour tends to be irresponsible and unpredictable. The patient's mood tends to be shallow and inappropriate to the circumstances, often accompanied by giggling or self-satisfied smiling, together with a peculiar manner, grimaces and pranks. Thoughts seem disorganized and speech is rambling and difficult to follow.

——— CATATONIC SCHIZOPHRENIA

Disturbances of movement are the main abnormality and alternate between extremes of excitement and stupor or mutism, and automatic obedience of instructions versus apparently negative responses to instructions. Strange or symbolic body postures (the arms outstretched like a crucifix, for example) may be maintained for long periods of time. Episodes of extreme excitement can occur. Catatonic schizophrenia is now rarely seen in the Western world, but is still observed in some developing countries.

——— UNDIFFERENTIATED SCHIZOPHRENIA

This category refers to illnesses meeting the criteria for schizophrenia, but not conforming to any one of the above subtypes, or showing the features of more than one subtype.

——— SIMPLE SCHIZOPHRENIA

Simple schizophrenia is difficult to diagnose. It is an uncommon condition in which there is slowly worsening 'odd' conduct, an inability to cope, and a decline in good behaviour. The illness is less obviously 'schizophrenic' than other subtypes and the negative symptoms that develop are not preceded by obvious acute symptoms. Following the development of negative symptoms, the patient may become apathetic and aimless, and vagrancy may result.

RESIDUAL SCHIZOPHRENIA

This is a chronic stage in the development of a schizophrenic illness in which there has been clear progression from an early stage, with acute symptoms, to a later stage, with long-term, negative symptoms. Usually, the patient is underactive in thought and behaviour, has a 'flat' mood, is passive and lacks initiative. There is little speech, poor communication and a 'flat' facial expression, together with poor eye-contact, poor self-care and poor social interaction. Dementia or other organic brain disease, chronic depression and institutionalization should all be excluded as causes of the negative symptoms before residual schizophrenia is diagnosed.

POST-SCHIZOPHRENIC DEPRESSION

Post-schizophrenic depression is a depressive illness that may be prolonged, which arises after a schizophrenic illness, some of the symptoms of which may still be present. The depressive symptoms are rarely severe or extensive enough to meet the criteria for a severe depressive episode, and it is often difficult to decide whether the patient's symptoms are down to the depression, medication, or the negative symptoms of the schizophrenia itself. Post-schizophrenic depression is associated with an increased risk of suicide.

Schizo-affective disorders

These are episodic illnesses in which both altered mood and symptoms of schizophrenia are present at the same time. Some patients have recurrent schizo-affective illnesses, which may be of the manic or depressive type, or a mixture of the two. Others have one or two schizo-affective illnesses interspersed between typical bouts of mania or depression. Although having components of two illnesses may be thought of as particularly distressing, patients who suffer from recurrent schizo-affective illness, particularly those whose symptoms are of the manic, rather than the depressive type, usually make a full recovery.

MANIC TYPE

Schizophrenic and manic symptoms are present in the same episode of illness. The mood usually takes the form of elation, accompanied by increased self-esteem and grandiose ideas. However, sometimes excitement or irritability are more obvious and may be accompanied by aggressive behaviour and persecutory ideas. There is increased energy, over-activity, impaired concentration, and a loss of normal social inhibition. Delusions of reference, grandeur or persecution may be present, but other, more typically schizophrenic, symptoms are required to make the diagnosis. Manic type schizo-affective disorders are usually florid with an acute onset. Behaviour is often grossly disturbed but, with treatment, full recovery generally occurs within a few weeks.

─────── DEPRESSIVE TYPE

Schizophrenic and depressive symptoms are present in the same episode of illness. Depressed mood is usually accompanied by symptoms such as slow thought, speech and movement; insomnia; loss of energy, appetite or weight; a reduction in normal interests; impaired concentration; guilt; feelings of hopelessness and suicidal thoughts. Other, more typically schizophrenic, symptoms are present; patients may insist that their thoughts are being broadcast or interfered with, or that alien forces are trying to control them. They may be convinced that they are being either spied on or plotted against.

Schizo-affective episodes of the depressive type are usually less dramatic than schizo-affective episodes of the manic type, but they tend to last longer and the outlook is less favourable. Although most patients recover completely with treatment, some eventually experience lasting impairment.

─────── **Recent concepts of schizophrenia**

Recent research has shown that the symptoms of schizophrenia may actually be classified into three groups, rather than the traditional two (according to positive and negative symptoms). The three new categories are psychomotor poverty, disorganization and reality distortion; these are summarized in the table below.

Category	Main symptoms
(1) Psychomotor poverty	Poverty of speech Blank facial expression Reduced amount of natural movement Reduced change of tone in speech Reduced emotional responsiveness
(2) Disorganization	Mood is out of keeping with situation Incoherent speech
(3) Reality distortion	Delusions, hallucinations

─────── **References**

ICD-10 (1992): Classification of Mental and Behavioural Disorders. Clinical descriptions and diagnostic guidelines. Geneva: World Health Organization, 1992.

DSM-IV (1994): Diagnostic and Statistical Manual of Mental Disorders. Washington DC: American Psychiatric Association, 1994.

Frangou S, Murray R. *Schizophrenia.* London: Martin Dunitz, 1997.

2 What causes schizophrenia?

Schizophrenia is a brain disorder

It used to be thought that schizophrenia was a 'functional' disorder, by which it was meant that there was no sign of brain disease or brain damage in schizophrenia, as there was in 'organic' disorders such as Alzheimer's disease and head injury cases, for example. All sorts of psychological and social theories were put forward in the past to explain why some people developed schizophrenia. Some psychoanalysts suggested that certain patterns of parenting and upbringing could confuse children so much that they develop-

ed schizophrenia in later life. There was really no scientific basis for such theories, which seemed not only to blame parents but to cause them unnecessary self-doubt and feelings of guilt. Unsurprisingly, this didn't help the parent–doctor relationship, nor the relationship between the parents and their afflicted child.

It is now well-established, however, that abnormalities in the structure and function of the brain are present in most people who suffer from schizophrenia. Post-mortem studies first suggested that the brains of people with schizophrenia were slightly smaller than usual and had abnormally large ventricles (the ventricles being the fluid-filled spaces in the middle of the brain). Over the past 20 years, these differences have been confirmed by studies of brain scans — both computerized tomography (CT) scans and magnetic resonance imaging (MRI) scans.

> ■ Abnormalities in structure and function are present in the brains of people with schizophrenia

These changes in the brain are subtle and amount to a reduction of only about 5% in the total amount of brain tissue. There is a big overlap, in general, between the brain size of people with schizophrenia and that of the rest of the population. Although the changes in schizophrenic patients are not so severe that their memory or intelligence level is affected significantly, they do seem to be the prime cause of the distressing symptoms and behavioural problems described in Chapter 1. Because the changes are so slight, and easily missed in any individual case, brain scans cannot be used to diagnose schizophrenia.

Research into the causes of these changes in schizophrenia is in progress. It has been known for many years now that there is a genetic factor in the disorder; in other words, that schizophrenia tends to run in some families. However, this is not the whole story, since factors in the environment also seem to be important.

Genetic factors

The chances of a person developing schizophrenia are increased if there is already someone in the family with the disorder. Risks are higher if a very close relative has schizophrenia, but not much higher than those of the general population if schizophrenia is only present in an uncle, aunt, or cousin.

Schizophrenia could be more common in certain families because relatives are more likely to share a similar upbringing. However, when the child of someone with schizophrenia is adopted by another family, the increased risk does not go away, proving that schizophrenia is carried in their genes and cannot be explained simply as a result of being brought up in a particular way.

It is unlikely that a single abnormal gene is responsible for schizophrenia — several genes are probably involved. Research on chromosomes is in progress and this might lead to the discovery of these genes in the next few years. However, it is unlikely to lead to new ways of treating schizophrenia in the foreseeable future.

The genetic contribution to schizophrenia

Affected relative	Risk of schizophrenia
Identical twin	46%
Non-identical twin	16%
Parent	14%
Sibling	9%
Grandparent	6%
Uncle or aunt	4%
Cousin	2%
No affected relative	1%

It is important to remember that, although the risk of schizophrenia in the child of a sufferer is increased to 14%, or one in seven, this still means that six out of seven children will *not* develop the disorder. Similarly, while the brother or sister (known as the 'sibling') of a sufferer has an increased risk of 9%, this still means that more than nine out of 10 siblings will *not* develop schizophrenia. Overall, more than 60% of people with schizophrenia have no close family history of the disorder. What is inherited is not a certainty of developing the disorder but a 'tendency' to do so — actual development is then dependent on other factors acting as the person themself develops.

Early brain development and schizophrenia

When the brains of people with schizophrenia have been studied under the microscope, the kinds of changes seen in the tissues suggest to the experts that the problem actually starts many years before schizophrenia develops in young adult life. In fact, it is likely that problems occur during the very early stages of brain development, either in the developing foetus (embryo) or around the time of birth. This has prompted researchers to look for possible causes of interference with brain development in people with schizophrenia — right back to the time that they were in their mother's womb, as well as the circumstances surrounding their birth.

VIRUS INFECTIONS AND SCHIZOPHRENIA

It has been noted for some time that people with schizophrenia are more likely to have been born in the winter or early spring than in the summer or autumn months. This suggested to some researchers that viral infections, which are more frequent in the winter, might have affected schizophrenia sufferers while they were still being carried in their mothers' wombs. In 1957, there was a severe epidemic of the virus infection influenza ('flu), and researchers in Helsinki later found that schizophrenia was more common among the children

of women who would have been six to nine months' pregnant at the time of the 'flu epidemic. However, the increased risk was slight and, at most, could explain only about one in 20 cases of the disorder. It seemed to be more of a factor among women sufferers of schizophrenia than men.

BIRTH DIFFICULTIES

A number of studies have found that a past history of birth difficulties or obstetric complications is more common among people with schizophrenia. Such difficulties and complications include difficult deliveries — perhaps involving forceps or Caesarian section, breathing problems at birth, and other complications that might have increased the risk of damage to the baby's brain. Again, such problems could only explain a small proportion of schizophrenia cases. They seem to be more of a factor among male sufferers of schizophrenia than women.

Developmental problems during childhood

If schizophrenia-related damage to the brain occurs in the womb or at the time of birth, it seems likely that people who eventually go on to develop schizophrenia might have problems during their childhood. There is some evidence that excessive anxiety and difficult behaviour are more likely among children who later go on to develop schizophrenia. Some researchers also believe that subtle disorders of movement and co-ordination may be present before the full illness develops. These problems, if indeed they are present, are not easy to spot. It is certainly not possible to tell from a child's movement or behaviour whether that child is at increased risk of developing schizophrenia as a teenager or young adult. Most children with anxiety or difficult behaviour will *not* develop schizophrenia, even if they have a relative with the disorder.

THE NEURODEVELOPMENTAL HYPOTHESIS

The theory outlined above, involving damage to the brain very early in development, many years before the onset of severe schizophrenic symptoms, is known as the *neurodevelopmental hypothesis*. It may explain other observations about schizophrenia, including the fact that this disorder is more likely in a person whose mother suffered from malnutrition during her pregnancy. Schizophrenia is also more common among young people born and brought up in the middle of cities. This may be due to the increased risk of catching a virus infection in more overcrowded living conditions.

Diet and the brain

■ Recent research has shown that diet may play a role in schizophrenia

The human body is made up of millions of tiny cells, which are grouped together to make 'tissues' (skin, fat, muscles, or tendons, for example). One or more tissues combine to make 'organs' (the heart, liver, kidney, or brain, for example). The human brain is the most complex and delicate organ, made up of specialized nerve cells (called neurones) which are supported and supplied by a variety of helper cells (called glia). Neurones are highly specialized for carrying electrical information, either within the brain, or further afield (eg, to the hands or feet). All cells, and especially neurones, depend on a good surrounding 'membrane' in order to function well. If the membrane is damaged the cell may not function properly (or die) and in the case of nerve cells, this means that information may not be relayed properly.

All cell membranes are made up of a double layer of special fatty molecules (lipids), forming something like a fine sheet. Scientists have discovered that, in schizophrenia, as well as certain other nerve diseases, there are some defects in the way the body actually makes the lipids that form the membranes of the nerve cells. Because nerve cells are delicate and highly specialized, they are very sensitive to minor structural problems. It is also thought that an absence of certain kinds of fat (eg, fish oil) in the diet may lead to poor nerve function in cells already damaged during development, and that this, in turn, may affect the course of schizophrenia. Thus, while a poor diet might affect the course of schizophrenia, it will not actually cause the illness.

Possible environmental causes of schizophrenia

- Virus infection of the developing baby in the womb
- Malnutrition of the mother during pregnancy
- Birth difficulties and complications
- Being born and raised in the inner city

■ All the research that has been done so far is consistent in one respect: there is no evidence that schizophrenia can be blamed on a person's parents or upbringing. There is no way at present of predicting which children might go on to develop schizophrenia. Therefore, there is no way of preventing an increased risk in some young people

Triggers of schizophrenia

We have seen that there are certain *underlying causes* of schizophrenia, including genes and brain development in early life, and yet the illness usually shows itself during adolescence or early adulthood. It seems that the illness is 'waiting to happen', but that something actually brings it on. Factors that bring on an episode of illness are called *'precipitating factors'*, and these are often triggers in the environment.

STRESS AND WORRY

Studies of the events around the time of the initial development of schizophrenia have shown that the illness often starts after a stressful time or an unhappy event in the person's life. This might be the loss of a job, bereavement in the family, the break-up of a relationship, or worries about finances or accommodation. An early sign of schizophrenia may be worry about such problems, which seems out of all proportion to those closest to the sufferer. This can be apparent for some time before more serious symptoms develop, such as hallucinations or delusions (see Chapter 1).

These life events and difficulties would not be sufficient to cause serious psychiatric illness in themselves, unless the person already had an underlying tendency to develop schizophrenia.

DRUGS AND ALCOHOL

Sometimes the onset of schizophrenia seems to be related to drinking too much alcohol. Again, drinking too much does not cause schizophrenia by itself. It is simply a precipitating factor (ie, trigger), that leads to significant illness only in those in whom the underlying tendency to develop schizophrenia is already present.

Misuse of some drugs has been found to lead to illnesses which are very similar to schizophrenia, with symptoms such as delusions, hallucinations, and disturbed behaviour. In particular, this type of problem can result from the use of stimulants such as *amphetamines* ('speed', 'whizz', 'uppers', 'sulphate') and *cocaine* ('coke', 'snow', 'crack', 'freebase', 'base'). These illnesses, known as *drug-induced psychoses*, are usually short-lived, perhaps lasting only a few days or weeks at the most. However, if the afflicted person has an underlying predisposition or vulnerability to schizophrenia, they may not recover so quickly and instead go on to develop the full illness and its longer-term problems.

Precipitating causes of schizophrenia

- Adverse life events
  losing a job, bereavement, the break-up of a relationship, etc
- Alcohol misuse
  (more than two drinks a day)
- Drugs
  Stimulants (amphetamines, cocaine)
  Hallucinogenics (LSD, magic mushrooms, angel dust)

Other drugs can cause hallucinations while they are taken, but the effects wear off almost immediately and the drugs do not lead to psychotic illness. These hallucinogenic drugs include *lysergic acid diethylamide* ('LSD' or 'acid'), *magic mushrooms* ('liberty caps' or 'fly agaric'), and *phencyclidine* ('PCP' or 'angel dust').

Anyone who has suffered from schizophrenia should ideally avoid drinking too much alcohol (one or two drinks a day, and preferably only at the weekend). They should also avoid taking any stimulant or hallucinogenic drugs whatsoever, if they are to reduce the risk of having a relapse of their illness.

—— Advice for Carers: expressed emotion

Expressed emotion is a term that was first used by researchers in the 1960s to describe a certain kind of human interaction to do simply with how people show their feelings to one another. It is normal to show feelings to other people, especially those close to us, but, in some situations, people may show too much emotion (positive or negative) for others to cope with. Such expression of emotion is known as 'high expressed emotion'.

- *High expressed emotion* includes *critical remarks* and *hostility* towards the schizophrenia sufferer, but also expressions of *emotional over-involvement*, with over-protectiveness, high expectations of close contact and demonstrations of affection that the other person may be unable to return

Studies going back to the 1960s have shown that high expressed emotion in a carer can increase the risk of relapse for the schizophrenia patient. High expressed emotion may double the risk of relapse in the first year after recovery from an episode of schizophrenic illness. In fact, when it comes to avoiding relapse, avoiding high expressed emotion is as important a factor for the schizophrenic patient as continuing to take medication.

It is not surprising that family members or other carers may develop a whole range of emotional responses to a person with schizophrenia. The affected person's behaviour may be socially disruptive, embarrassing, or frustrating, and carers may feel a number of mixed emotions: anger at such behaviour; guilt because the person is ill; grief at seeming to lose the person they used to know before the illness struck; worry about how they will manage; and isolation from the rest of the world. The negative symptoms of schizophrenia are particularly difficult to understand and forgive, and may be interpreted as laziness, which is not usually the case. However, if the carer expresses such emotions to the sufferer, it will often only serve to increase their anxiety and make relapse more likely.

Carers may need considerable time and professional help to learn how best to deal with sufferers. They will need to find the right balance between allowing the person with schizophrenia the time and space they need to be alone, while encouraging a reasonable level of day-to-day activity and social contact. Some expressions of warmth and support (without overdoing it) have been shown to be helpful to sufferers, but these may have to be given without any great expectation of similar expressions returned.

How to live with someone with schizophrenia

- Give them space and time alone if they need it
- Encourage some activity and socializing every day
- Try to avoid criticizing them (not at all easy sometimes)
- Try to avoid overprotection or smothering with kindness
- Try to accept that they may not be able to return expressions of love or gratitude to the same degree
- Try to offer them warmth and support
- Seek professional advice if tensions are running high

Avoiding high levels of expressed emotion and finding the right balance between over- and under-stimulation is often not easy. Help, in the form of professional advice and support, and sometimes respite care, should always be available. These options are dealt with in later chapters.

Advice for sufferers: avoiding stress

Since stressful life events seem to precipitate schizophrenia, it is important, in order to try to avoid a relapse, that people who have recovered from a previous episode should try to reduce sources of stress in their lives.

Sometimes it may seem to those close to the sufferer that it would be best for their friend or family member to get back to work or college as soon as possible and to resume all the things in their life that had to stop while they were ill. However, going back to work, particularly to a stressful job, may lead to anxiety and increase the risk of relapse and it may be too much to expect (especially straight after an episode of schizophrenia) a sufferer to pick up where they left off, play a full part in life again, and fulfil the expectations of family, girlfriend or boyfriend, or employer.

Some people who have suffered from schizophrenia seem to want to spend much more time by themselves, perhaps being alone in their room for hours on end. And, in fact, if such people are forced to interact, they can find it so stressful that they develop more symptoms and suffer a relapse.

Conversely, if people with schizophrenia are not usefully employed in some activity on most days, then the *negative* symptoms of schizophrenia (see Chapter 1) can develop. Patients can become more withdrawn, very quiet, almost emotionless, and apathetic — not even bothering much about looking after themselves and their belongings.

This means that a *balance* between *overstimulation* — involving many activities, contact with others, and expectations of work and socializing, and *understimulation* — leaving the person to spend all day alone in their room, has to be struck.

PSYCHOSOCIAL INTERVENTION (PSI)

Families or other carers struggling to find this correct balance should be able to obtain help and advice from the psychiatrist, mental health nurse (community psychiatric nurse or CPN) or occupational therapist (OT), who are all members of the community mental health team. These professionals are particularly likely to want to discuss the way that the carer(s) should be talking to their patients — especially in terms of expressing emotion and feelings towards them. Psychosocial intervention addresses the problems of patients wth schizophrenia within their own social surroundings.

3 Medical treatment

Medical treatment usually refers to medication, but the doctors who treat people with mental health problems do not only use drugs. Such doctors are called psychiatrists, and they have a medical degree and further training in dealing with illnesses that affect the mind. Mental illness may mainly result from problems in the way people think (psychological), or from problems in the way their brain is functioning (organic). Since most psychiatric illnesses are a combin-  ation of both, however, psychiatrists are trained to use a combination of approaches, both medical and psychological, in order to achieve the best possible outcome for people with mental health problems. This Chapter will deal mainly with the physical aspects of treatment for schizophrenia — the rest will be covered later.

Since schizophrenia accounts for nearly 10% of the total NHS inpatient budget — more than any other illness, and with the current emphasis on care in the community, there is a real need both for better use of the wide range of schizophrenic treatments (this includes medication, talking treatments, other therapies and effective early intervention), and for better information and help for patients, carers and relatives. The more patients with schizophrenia are managed in the community, the more teamwork between general practitioners (GPs), psychiatrists and community mental health teams is required.

Effective early treatment improves the long-term outlook for people with schizophrenia. Most first episodes of this condition occur in adolescence or early adult life, and correct initial treatment is crucial. The symptoms of schizophrenia can be controlled by medication (drugs). However, the distressing and severe side-effects of some of the older drugs can cause some people to stop taking them — this is known as *non-compliance*, or non-adherence. Abandoning drug therapy almost always leads to relapse, and can result in hospital admission. Fortunately, the newer drugs are as effective in treating symptoms and have fewer side-effects and patients can be encouraged to stick to them, provided they and their family are supported and taught about the value of treatment.

Drug treatment

■ Drug treatment is an essential part of treatment

Drug treatment is best used to control acute psychotic symptoms and to prevent relapse in the longer-term. Drugs used in the treatment of schizophrenia are called antipsychotic drugs.

OLD VS NEW

There are older, conventional, antipsychotics and newer, atypical, antipsychotics. Examples of the older drugs include: chlorpromazine, thioridazine, fluphenazine, haloperidol, flupenthixol and pimozide. They are classified according to their different chemical structures, and all appear to work by blocking a chemical messenger, dopamine, at nerve endings in the brain. The older drugs tend to be associated with more side-effects (see page 20) than their newer counterparts, which are considered 'cleaner'. For a new drug to be classed as 'atypical', the general rule is that it should not produce unwanted effects on movement, nor on the hormone prolactin.

Antipsychotic drugs are intended to calm the patient without making them drowsy or causing excitement. They can relieve symptoms in most patients but, in some, the improvement is only partial. There tends to be more improvement in positive symptoms such as delusions and hallucinations than in negative symptoms such as social withdrawal and apathy. Older drugs have the potential to produce unwanted side-effects such as trembling, stillness, abnormal face and body movements, restlessness, and tardive dyskinesia (involuntary movements, usually facial, which generally occur after years of medication). Although many of these unwanted effects disappear if treatment is withdrawn or reduced or medication is given to counteract them, giving drugs routinely to stop side-effects is not justified:

- not all patients are affected by the side-effect
- in some cases, the side-effects may be worsened
- newer drugs produce fewer side-effects.

Acute treatment

■ Drug treatment with antipsychotic medication should be started as soon as possible once an accurate diagnosis has been made

Any delay could mean a less positive outcome in the long term. Although a patient's overall behaviour is likely to improve quickly with drug treatment, some acute symptoms of illness may take weeks or even months to disappear completely. Some drugs (eg, chlorpromazine) are more sedative than others, for example, which may be a benefit or a drawback depending on the specific circumstances, while others (eg, depixol) are considered to be more 'alerting'.

Medication generally takes several weeks to reach its full effect. If troublesome symptoms still persist after six weeks, either more of the drug in question may be given for a further short period, or a different class of antipsychotic drug may be tried instead. Additional benzodiazepine tranquillizers may help control symptoms in very disturbed and aggressive patients, and this may allow lower doses of antipsychotic medication to be used, with a lower risk of side-effects. Medication may need to be given by injection in an emergency, to restrain a patient who may be at risk of hurting themselves or others.

About one in 10 patients will remain permanently well after stopping drug treatment following a first episode of schizophrenia, but it is almost impossible to predict which patients will be in this 10% group.

Maintenance treatment

■ Because of the risk of relapse it is usually advised that medication is taken for years, sometimes for life

Continued (maintenance) treatment with antipsychotic medication reduces risk of relapse. After an acute illness, or even if treatment is withdrawn after years of successful maintenance treatment, patients relapse at a rate of about one in 10 for each month without medication. The relapse rate is halved in patients who continue their medication and continuous drug treatment is better than taking medication 'on and off'.

Factors that are important in deciding whether or not to continue or withdraw maintenance medication include: the risks to the patient if they relapse, the patient's ability to tolerate medication, the level of social support available, and the views of the patient, their relatives and carers.

DEPOT MEDICATION

Maintenance treatment may be given orally or by 'depot' injection, usually every two to four weeks, but sometimes less or more frequently. Depot injections are absorbed slowly and provide therapeutic levels of the drug (levels that work) between injections. If depot injections are given at depot clinics, there is also the opportunity for regular review and monitoring of, and contact with, the patient. Although injections are advantageous in that they usually remove the need for daily tablets, they can be painful and changing the site of injection at each visit is therefore sensible. If the patient is under stress or shows signs of relapse, the depot treatment should be supplemented with oral treatment as the depot will probably not work quickly enough in this situation. Depot treatment is best for patients treated in the community, since they may not take oral treatment, resulting in readmission to hospital.

Unwanted side-effects

■ Unwanted side-effects are common, but usually a nuisance rather than a serious problem

If side-effects are making it difficult for the patient to take their medication, they must tell their doctor. A change to a different, better suited, medication can probably be arranged. The main side-effects of antipsychotic medication are listed below:

EXTRAPYRAMIDAL EFFECTS

The term extrapyramidal refers to nerve pathways in the brain and body that control a person's natural flow of movement and also body posture (involuntarily or uncons-ciously controlled). Old fashioned ('conventional') antipsychotics like haloperidol can cause stiffness and trembling, like that seen in Parkinson's disease. This gives rise to the term 'parkinsonian side-effects', which occur in about a third of patients taking conventional drugs and which can be treated with anti-parkinsonian drugs (eg, benzhexol, benztropine, orphenadrine, and procyclidine).

ACUTE DYSTONIC REACTIONS

Acute dystonia refers to the sudden onset of stiffness and rigidity, which is sometimes accompanied by eye-rolling. This is both painful and distressing, but can be treated, rapidly, with anti-parkinsonian drugs — the latter may need to be given by injection.

AKATHISIA

This is a distressing sensation of inner restlessness, which leads to constant motion; a sufferer may sit down, then stand up, then sit down again and again, for example, or constantly walk up and down a room, unable to settle for more than a few moments at a time. This side-effect can sometimes be mistaken for the agitation of acute illness, and is treatable with drugs called 'beta-blockers' (which are sometimes also used to treat high blood pressure).

TARDIVE DYSKINESIA

This term refers to uncontrollable movements, initially affecting the face, lips and tongue, so that the sufferer makes strange lip-smacking and sucking noises. It tends to occur after many years of taking conventional antipsychotics, and is very difficult to treat and a distressing and unsightly side-effect. It affects up to 20% of patients taking conventional antipsychotics long term, 10% of whom are severely affected. The risk is higher in older patients. Sometimes, tardive dyskinesia also occurs in people who have had schizophrenia for many years, but who have never taken any medication. To limit the occurrence of tardive dyskinesia, antipsychotic drugs — preferably newer ('atypical') antipsychotic drugs — should be used at the lowest possible doses.

MUSCARINIC SIDE-EFFECTS

Muscarinic side-effects refer to the effects of drugs on the specialized nerves that our bodies use to deal with emergency situations. These include: dry mouth, blurred vision, constipation, difficulty passing water, confusion and a fast heart rate.

ANTI-ADRENERGIC EFFECTS

Anti-adrenergic side-effects refer to the effects of drugs on the specialized nerves that control blood pressure. These side-effects can lead to dizziness if the sufferer stands up quickly.

ANTIHISTAMINERGIC EFFECTS

Antihistaminic side-effects refer to the effects of drugs on the specialized nerves that control levels of alertness. They can lead to drowsiness, which is often troublesome, especially in older people, and weight gain.

Unwanted side-effects: a summary

Extrapyramidal effects	Stiffness, slow movements and sometimes trembling
Acute dystonic reactions	Sudden onset of stiffness and rigidity
Akathisia	Inner restlessness and constant moving around
Tardive dyskinesia	Uncontrollable movements of face, lips and tongue
Muscarinic side effect	Dry mouth, blurred vision, constipation, difficulty passing water
Anti-adrenergic effects	Dizziness when standing up quickly
Antihistaminergic effects	Drowsiness, weight gain

PROLACTOGENIC EFFECTS

Some drugs increase levels of the hormone prolactin in the body, which can lead to swelling of the breasts and milk production — in men as well as women. Increased prolactin levels may also cause impotence in men and stop menstrual periods in women.

NEUROLEPTIC MALIGNANT SYNDROME

Neuroleptic malignant syndrome is a dramatic, rare, at times fatal, reaction seen most commonly early in treatment. Typical features are muscular rigidity, raised temperature, fluctuating consciousness and an unstable blood pressure and heart rate. Treatment in a hospital intensive care unit will be needed.

OTHER (RARE) EFFECTS

Other, rare, side-effects of drug treatment include weight gain, convulsions, jaundice, lowering of the white blood cell count, skin sensitivity to sunlight, contact dermatitis and rashes and sexual dysfunction — in both men and women. Additionally, chlorpromazine or thioridazine use may lead to pigmentation of the skin, cornea or lens. Antipsychotic drugs cross the placenta of pregnant women and are present in breast milk. If antipsychotic medication is needed by women during pregnancy or breastfeeding, it should be given in the lowest possible doses.

There have been rare reports of sudden death occurring in people on antipsychotic medication, but a direct link is not proven and the risk is not fully understood. All medicines have potentially serious effects and it is always a case of balancing the risks against the benefits: it is the authors' opinion that the benefits of antipsychotic drugs far outweigh the side-effects.

The abrupt withdrawal of antipsychotic drugs occasionally produces feelings of sickness, abdominal pain, diarrhoea, restlessness and sleep problems; it may also worsen involuntary movements. Therefore, all doses should be reduced gradually.

SIDE-EFFECT ADVICE

Fortunately, the newer drugs do not seem to have such dramatic side-effects as the older drugs. Nevertheless, some do cause side-effects, such as stiffness and weight gain. In every case, the most important issue for the patient and carer is to discuss all side effects with their doctor. The main aim of medical treatment is to use the smallest dose of drug possible in order to keep the symptoms of schizophrenia at bay, at the same time avoiding or minimizing any side-effects of treatment. It is extremely important that the patient does not simply stop taking their medication without seeking their doctor's advice on either reducing the dose or changing to a different antipsychotic. This may lead to relapse, which is not only very distressing in itself, but may require high doses of conventional antipsychotics to retreat the acute symptoms, with all the unpleasant side-effects already mentioned. In other words, the patient, far from avoiding unwanted side-effects, will end up needing more of the drugs that caused them in the first place.

Interactions with other drugs

Alcohol and sedative medication increase drowsiness in people taking antipsychotic treatment. In addition, the older, established antidepressant drugs increase the blood levels of antipsychotic drugs and this may put patients at risk of heart irregularities. Antipsychotic drugs can complicate treatment with anti-epilepsy drugs and lead to seizures. Antipsychotic drugs taken with lithium, a mood-stabilizing drug, may lead to excitation, restlessness, muscle rigidity, and raised body temperature.

Compliance (adherence/alliance)

Poor compliance with treatment is common and is an important cause of relapse in schizophrenia. It occurs in a third of inpatients and two-thirds of patients in the community. There are several reasons why patients abandon their treatments, or fail to comply with them. They may have received inadequate information on them, experienced difficulty in managing the treatment doses, be in denial of their illness, or simply forgetful. Some patients do not feel well on their medication, or see the benefits of it — even though their symptoms may have improved. The unwanted side-effects of medication, especially stiffness and involuntary movements, are most likely to put patients off their medication. In order to avoid non-compliance, both patients and carers need to know the nature and purpose of their treatment, including any possible unwanted side-effects associated with it. GPs and psychiatrists are able to provide this information.

It also helps if the simplest possible treatment regimen is applied. The patient should be observed for, and questioned specifically about, unwanted side-effects, which may be lessened by reducing drug dose or by changing to a better tolerated drug.

Depression

Over half of all patients with schizophrenia have depressive symptoms during their acute illness, and a quarter to a half experience them during their recovery phase. Depression may be difficult to distinguish from the negative symptoms of schizophrenia, and from some drug-induced side-effects that make the patient seem depressed. Antidepressant medication is effective for the treatment of depression in people with schizophrenia.

Treatment resistance

Some patients seem resistant to treatment. Treatment resistance is defined as failure to achieve satisfactory symptom relief, despite the trial of at least three different types of antipsychotic, each given at the correct dosages for at least six weeks. Factors to do with the patient's social situation that might aggravate acute symptoms — eg, high levels of stress or the use of illicit drugs — should be considered. Patients who are not taking their medication as prescribed, or who require a higher or lower dose of their antipsychotic drug, can be identified by measuring the levels of the relevant drug in their blood. It should be noted that higher doses of any particular drug will not solve the problem of treatment resistance, but that changing to a different drug can help to overcome it. Lithium, a mood stabilizer, and lorazepam, a tranquillizer, both seem to improve the effectiveness of antipsychotic drugs, particularly where there are additional symptoms of mood disorder or anxiety. Carbamazepine, another mood stabilizer, and propranolol, for symptoms of anxiety, have also been used in this situation.

CLOZAPINE TREATMENT

Most (70% of) treatment-resistant cases of schizophrenia respond to a drug called clozapine. Although it was introduced into Europe in the 1960s, there were, unfortunately, some fatal side-effects, which led to it being withdrawn from most western countries. It has recently been re-introduced, with strict safeguards. Positive and negative symptoms, behaviour and social function all improve with clozapine, while excess salivation, drowsiness, weight gain, and a fast heart rate are unwanted side-effects, and convulsions may occur. Involuntary movements are rare, though, and established tardive dyskinesia (see page 19) may even improve on clozapine treatment. The most serious unwanted side-effect of this drug is a reduced number of white blood cells in the blood (agranulocytosis); since white blood cells help to defend the body against infection, patients are therefore at risk of serious infection. Agranulocytosis occurs approximately 10 times more frequently with clozapine than with older, established antipsychotic drugs and, for this reason, its use is restricted to patients who are registered with the Clozaril Patient Monitoring Service (this ensures regular monitoring of white blood cell counts and treatment is stopped if the white cell count falls below a standard level).

Antipsychotic drugs: a summary

'Conventional' antipsychotics (tablets and syrup)

Benperidol	Pimozide	Prochlorperazine
Dihydrochloride	Droperidol	Promazine
Flupenthixol	Chlorpromazine	Fluphenazine
Perphenazine	Haloperidol	Sulpiride
Loxapine	Thioridazine	Methotrimeprazine
Trifluoperazine	Zuclopenthixol	Pericyazine
Oxypertine		

Antipsychotic depot preparations (injections)

Flupenthixol decanoate
Fluphenazine decanoate
Haloperidol decanoate
Pipothiazine palmitate
Zuclopenthixol decanoate

Newer (or 'atypical') drugs

Newer drugs tend to act in a different way (affecting different chemical messengers) than the older drugs and so are less likely to cause side-effects and can help negative symptoms. Some of the newer atypical, drugs require blood pressure monitoring during the early stages of treatment. The atypical antipsychotics include:

Risperidone
Olanzapine
Quetiapine
Clozapine

4 The family, community and other treatments

Medication treats acute and some negative symptoms of schizophrenia but does not always give a complete cure. The support of family and friends, community care, 'talking treatments' and rehabilitation are all essential too. A 'care package' consisting of all the elements that help an individual is the aim.

Family and friends

Family and friends are not the cause of schizophrenia. When someone you love has schizophrenia many questions and powerful emotions are expressed: blame, guilt, anger, worry, desperation and disbelief — and there is also the sense of isolation and of being stigmatized.

> ■ Family and friends need support, information and advice, but are frequently left to shoulder the burden alone, and often feel that no-one understands or cares

The general practitioner, members of the local mental health team and voluntary groups are far more able to give support to people with schizophrenia and their carers than in the past, and are ready to respond to individual concerns and crises.

Helping or caring for a loved one is a task that may need to continue for years and can be draining as well as rewarding. Family relationships and friendships will change because of the effect schizophrenia has on communication, closeness and behaviour. Also, a carer may unexpectedly have to become the sole provider for the family, with all that that entails, in addition to encouraging the sufferer in all manner of day-to-day activities: making friends, taking up interests and hobbies, washing, shopping and using the telephone.

Coping

> ■ Carers need to learn as much as they can about schizophrenia and its treatment, including how to recognize warning signs and who to turn to for help when it is needed

Caring for someone with schizophrenia sometimes means learning the hard way. Experience will show that some ideas work while others don't. The simplest advice is to keep trying those things that do work and to avoid those that don't.

DEALING WITH FRUSTRATION

Problems need to be tackled calmly and one at a time. Pushing too hard can create stress that may worsen the patient's symptoms. In times of acute illness it may be appropriate for the carer to become closely involved, but at other times 'doing too much' can be counterproductive and hinder the patient's efforts to try out their own skills and to gain much-needed confidence in even the simplest tasks and chores. The balance is not easy to achieve for the carer. Above all, they should try to remember that — although progress may seem slow and there may be many setbacks — it is small steps in the right direction that make the journey to recovery.

STRESS

> ■ If there is too much stress at home and the whole family is suffering, a solution that may have to be considered is living apart from the sufferer, while maintaining regular contact

People with schizophrenia are usually badly affected by family stress. Expressions of stress that are particularly harmful are: many critical comments about the person with schizophrenia; hostility or anger towards the person with schizophrenia; and overly emotional involvement with the person with schizophrenia.

Family-based 'talking treatments' teach carers how to avoid these traps and cut down the number of relapses, but they are not available everywhere — you may have to ask your doctor. When it comes to talking to the sufferer, overstimulation and under-stimulation can be equally damaging.

LOOKING AFTER YOURSELF, DIET AND EXERCISE

The symptoms of schizophrenia can clearly limit a patient's lifestyle (eg, the patient may be less motivated to look after themselves or to socialize). In addition, some of the medication used to treat this illness may restrict the patient in other ways; there may be some weight gain, drowsiness, constipation, or impotence, for example. These problems can be countered by adopting the following simple lifestyle changes (your GP will be able to advise further, if necessary):

- Regular exercise (20 minutes of a raised heart rate three times a week) such as jogging, cycling, swimming or even a brisk daily walk, will help you feel better. Research has shown marked benefits from sensible exercise in a number of medical conditions, including mental health.
- It is also advisable to cut down or give up smoking, as, again, scientific evidence has shown that smoking can make the symptoms of schizophrenia worse. You should certainly avoid using illicit drugs, in

particular stimulants such as amphetamines (speed and ecstasy).

● Try to eat healthily and avoid 'comfort eating'. If you are feeling a bit 'down', it might be a good time to go for a brisk walk instead. Try to increase the amount of fibre in your diet — ideally by eating more fruit and vegetables, since these also contain valuable vitamins. It is sensible to keep fatty foods to a minimum as these can make it harder for your body to absorb your medication. Indigestion remedies can also reduce the amount of antipsychotic medication your body absorbs. In other ways, it pays to cut down on caffeine, which is present in tea, coffee and many fizzy drinks such as cola. If you find it impossible to give up all of these things, then think about having them as treats or rewards, rather than all the time.

There are plenty of reasons to be hopeful even when things seem desperate. People with schizophrenia can get better after long illnesses and new drugs and talking treatments are being introduced all the time. Avoiding stress, keeping up your own interests and making the time to relax are all powerful means of protection and will give you extra strength. Every individual needs to progress at their own pace and no-one should try to achieve everything at once. A step at a time, and taking each day as it comes, are good pointers.

——— Community care

This is a term to love or hate. Community care has been known to produce results that really help sufferers and carers, but has also been known to fail dramatically. Its aim is to provide full local support for people with mental illness living at home.

What people should expect locally

● Involvement in choosing what care or treatment is offered
● Integration into the community and its activities
● Protection from abuse
● Periods of asylum, ie, peace and rest, when necessary
● Relief from distress
● To be noticed when in need
● Help with finances, housing, leisure and employment
● Help at any time around the clock
● Help for life, including help with medical and psychiatric treatment
● Protection with respect to legal matters

After leaving hospital the first person to turn to is usually the family doctor, who tends to be involved in both day-to-day medical problems and at times of crisis. Usually there will also be a keyworker, often a community psychiatric nurse, CPN, to coordinate care and form the link between the sufferer, the family, the general practitioner and the mental health team.

Apart from medical and psychiatric treatment, the main types of help for schizophrenia patients are:

- Discussing problems caused by disturbed behaviour and coming up with ways of improving that behaviour, or coping with it
- Discussing feelings and reactions to illness — sharing concerns and ideas can help to correct misunderstandings, allow better understanding of the patient, and a more realistic expectation of their illness and the future
- Contact with people who really do understand can reduce feelings of isolation and stigma. Other patients can be met in self-help and voluntary groups, for example, in which experiences, the latest information and support and understanding can be shared
- Churches, religious organizations and the police are usually very ready to help too

Talking treatments

There is currently great interest in what are known as 'talking treatments'. Several new types are being tried out. One of the problems with any schizophrenia treatment, but particularly talking treatments, is that schizophrenia patients often do not believe they are ill and are therefore unwilling to participate.

Most 'talking' work with patients and their families or carers aims to:

- Improve social and mental functioning
- Reduce the risk of relapse into illness
- Reduce the severity of symptoms
- Teach how to recognise and check on warning signs, and get help quickly
- Increase compliance with medication and treatment

Providing information, advice and practical support to patients and families is the main point of talking treatment. When a patient is experiencing acute symptoms, they need to feel that their carer believes that the symptoms are real and distressing for them — they do not need blunt dismissal or to be told that their symptoms are imaginary. Reassuring the sufferer that their symptoms, like delusions, are understood, despite not being shared, will help to build trust.

Ways in which carers can help their loved ones include:

- Learning about the illness and its treatment, the side-effects, community care, and what is likely to happen in the future
- Reducing stress in the family by recognizing things that cause stress and avoiding them
- Increasing the patient's independence at a comfortable pace
- Tackling day-to-day problems by trying out practical solutions one at a time and observing the effects
- Family work — this is not yet universally available, but community psychiatric nurses are increasingly being trained to help families cope better with illness within them. In particular, families are shown ways of interacting with their ill loved one in ways that help the patient. This is sometimes referred to as psychosocial intervention (PSI)

Cognitive behavioural methods

The term 'cognitive' simply refers to the way we think, and 'behaviour' to the way we act. Hence, cognitive–behavioural therapy is aimed at changing the ways we think and behave. It can help lessen acute symptoms and distress in schizophrenia patients by the following means:

- encouraging helpful ways of thinking about the illness
- distracting attention from the acute symptoms (like hearing voices)
- altering beliefs due to the illness (such as delusions)
- reducing stress in a number of ways, such as inducing relaxation.

Research is taking place to see if such talking treatments can be successful alone or are better used in combination with medication.

Rehabilitation

People with schizophrenia who have been in hospital do not all take the same length of time to re-adjust to their new situation and, for some of those discharged from hospital, independence may seem an unrealistic goal. Each individual will have different needs.

However, advances in medical and talking treatments, together with good community support, is increasingly allowing people with schizophrenia to live satisfying lives outside the hospital setting. The range of accommodation options is wide:

- hostel wards
- hospital houses
- hostels with varying degrees of supervision
- staffed and unstaffed grouped homes
- supported lodgings
- independent flats.

Simultaneously, outpatient care and therapy may be given at: home, the day hospital, day centres, drop-in centres, outpatient clinics, resource centres, and the GP surgery.

ACTIVITY

In terms of activity and exercise, people with schizophrenia should also be able to progress at their own pace, starting with simple individual activities, and, only as they gain confidence and improve, moving back to a 'normal' working lifestyle.

Activities will include: physical activity such as keep-fit, recreation, occupational therapy, sheltered workshop activities, and, eventually, paid employment.

> ■ Most people with schizophrenia want to work and do work when they are not ill

Other methods

There are many other types of therapy, from psychoanalysis to 'primal scream therapy', and most of these are not particularly helpful for most people with schizophrenia — some may even do more harm than good. The same is probably true of complementary therapies, such as acupuncture, aromatherapy and herbal remedies. It is always best to talk to the patient's general practitioner or keyworker before starting on something that may cost a lot of money and do no good.

5   Getting help

Sometimes people with loved ones who appear to be mentally unwell find it hard to get help. This is frequently because the loved one does not realize that they are ill and therefore refuses to accept that they need help. The friends and family of people with schizophrenia often sense that something is wrong, while the sufferers themselves lack the insight to appreciate that their experiences are the result of mental illness.

The general practitioner is the first port of call

Everyone in the UK has the right to be registered with a general practitioner (GP), except people who have been in hospital for more than a year. People who move around from place to place may register with an NHS GP wherever they are at any particular time, for three months at a time, as a 'temporary resident'.

> ■   It is best to take mental health problems to your GP rather than going straight to a hospital casualty department or psychiatric ward

Your GP will usually provide some treatment straight away, or refer the patient on to a specialist, or both. He or she will know the right person to refer the patient on to. In contrast, if the mental health problem is not thought to be immediately urgent, a casualty doctor may simply send the patient away again.

HOME VISITS

The GP will visit the patient at home if necessary, if, for example, they won't come to the surgery because they don't agree that they need help. It is more time-consuming for the GP to make a home visit (four people can be seen in surgery in the same time it takes to visit one patient), however, and the equipment and facilities available in the surgery are obviously not available in the patient's home.

For these reasons it is better, if possible, that the patient makes a surgery appointment to see the doctor. However, the doctor can be asked to make a home visit and cannot refuse to visit a registered patient in need of such help as long as that patient is staying at an address within the doctor's practice area (usually the same town as the doctor's surgery).

THE IMPORTANCE OF REGISTERING WITH A GP

If a person who is not already registered with a local doctor needs treatment in an emergency, then any GP must see that person as soon as possible, as long as the person is staying at an address within the GP's practice area. However, this only applies to real emergencies, in which somebody is seriously ill or at immediate risk of harming themselves or others.

The carer may have to insist that the GP sees the person, and stress that the situation is a true emergency, which serves to emphasize that it really is important for all people with schizophrenia to be registered with a GP. This is even more important for those about to leave hospital, who should see a GP within a few days of their discharge. At this stage, the GP will usually provide repeat prescriptions of the medication recommended by the specialist, and sickness certificates (sick notes) if necessary, as well as dealing with the patient's physical health problems.

WHAT IF AN ILL RELATIVE WON'T SEE THE GP?

As already mentioned, some people suffering from schizophrenia may not want help. This might be because bizarre beliefs (delusions) associated with their illness convince them, for example, that their problems are due to aliens from space, or admit that they are ill but say that previous experience of medical treatment (eg, the side-effects of some of the older drugs, see Chapter 3) has put them off. Whichever, the resulting lack of treatment may lead to their condition deteriorating to the point where carers and loved ones become very concerned, and where their thoughts and behaviour may put them and/or others at risk.

This is precisely the sort of situation in which a GP home visit should be requested. If the patient still refuses to see the GP, in their own home, and the GP forms the impression that this is because the patient is mentally ill, the GP may ask for a psychiatrist and social worker to try and see the patient, with a view to bringing them into hospital for a period of assessment. If the patient is still resistant at this stage, but is considered to be suffering from mental disorder, they may be brought into hospital against their wishes under the Mental Health Act (1983) (see Chapter 6).

Getting the best out of your GP

These days, all GPs should provide written details for patients of surgery times, how to go about making an appointment, how to ask for a repeat prescription, when the GP is and is not available to speak on the telephone, and how to request a home visit both during the day and 'out-of-hours' (in the evening or at weekends). The GP practice is also obliged to give details of how they handle complaints and suggestions. You should ask your GP's receptionist for the relevant practice leaflet or booklet and you will get the best out of your doctor by cooperating as much as possible with the information in it — ie, the surgery's arrangements for appointments, telephone calls and visits.

It will be appreciated if you arrive on time for your appointment. Also, if possible, try to make any requests for a home visit before 10 o'clock in the morning, which will enable the GP to plan his or her day around it more easily. Remember that you are only one of 40 or so patients the GP has to see every day, and that sometimes there is quite a lot of pressure to fit everybody in. The GP may be even more helpful if he or she feels that you have been helpful too.

It is also best, if you can, to keep the number of problems you want to talk about down to two or three at most for each appointment, since appointments are generally only allocated about 10 minutes each. The GP will, of course, see you for longer if you have a particularly difficult problem that needs more time, but each appointment that lasts for more than 10 minutes will make them later for all the other patients who are waiting to be seen. You can always make another appointment to deal with any problems not covered in the first consultation, but if you feel that these problems cannot wait, you might be able to request a 'double appointment' in one sitting, giving you enough time to discuss your current problems, worries, or complaints more fully.

Don't be afraid to write down a list of things you want to say, or questions you want to ask, when you go for your appointment. Although some doctors don't seem to like lists, they will usually go through each point and answer each question carefully, if asked. Nor should you be afraid to take along a friend, if you think this will make you feel less nervous or if you are worried that you won't be able to remember everything you need to say. People whose first language is not English may also like or need to take an interpreter along with them. However, practices in areas where there are many such non-English speakers often provide interpreters on request. Any such service, along with other services for ethnic minorities should, again, be written in the practice's patient information.

If you are unhappy with something the GP does or does not do for you, or for your relative or friend with schizophrenia, it is best if you try to have a quiet word with the doctor in question first. Many disagreements can be sorted out quickly by speaking either to the doctor or to the practice manager. Only if you feel that this has not worked, should you resort to an official complaint (see page 40).

Getting the best out of your GP

- Ask for the practice leaflet or booklet
- Cooperate with the arrangements for requesting appointments and visits as much as possible
- If you can, stick to one or two problems only at each consultation
- Make a list of your problems or questions to help you remember them
- Take along a friend or relative if you are nervous
- Ask for an interpreter if you need one
- Have a word with the doctor or practice manager if you have any problems, before making an official complaint

CHANGING YOUR GP

If you and your doctor simply cannot agree, or you cannot get on with your doctor, then you can change GPs by taking your NHS medical card along to another doctor's practice and asking to sign on there. If all the other local practices are full and say that they can't add you to their patient list, you must telephone the Primary Care Authority (formerly the Family Health Service Authority, or FHSA), the number of which is on your NHS medical card (and in the telephone book). The Primary Care Authority will find you a new GP within a few days at the most.

Similarly, GPs have the right to refuse to continue to treat someone whom they feel they cannot get on with. If a patient is abusive, aggressive, or violent with the doctor or with the doctor's staff, then the patient can be removed from the doctor's list straight away. However, if that patient is suffering from mental health problems, then the GP must address those mental health problems before the patient can be removed from the list. Effectively, this either means giving treatment or referring the patient to the mental health services for help.

Mental health service teams

Mental health professionals usually work in teams that include psychiatrists, mental health nurses, social workers, occupational therapists and psychologists. These team are usually called '*multidisciplinary community mental health teams*' or '*CMHT's*. Each of the different professionals involved has different qualifications and plays a different role within the team.

PSYCHIATRISTS

Psychiatrists are doctors who have completed six years in medical school learning about physical health care as well as mental health problems. They then spend several more years as specialists learning to look after mental health problems, working as 'senior house officers', 'registrars', or 'hospital practitioners', in mental hospital wards, psychiatric outpatient clinics, and community mental health teams. To become a 'consultant' psychiatrist, which is the most senior position available, they must have passed the examination for membership of the Royal College of Psychiatrists, and thus have the letters 'MRCPsych' after their names.

The psychiatrist's role within the CMHT is to make the diagnosis and decide on the treatment, often including medication such as tablets or injections. A psychiatrist is always involved when the patient needs admitting to hospital, whether voluntarily or under a Section of the Mental Health Act (see Chapter 6). The psychiatrist, like all the mental health professionals in the CMHT, will also spend time listening to the patient's problems and offering advice and support. The psychiatrist is usually, though not always, the team leader.

MENTAL HEALTH NURSES

Mental health nurses have a variety of roles. Qualified nurses who work in psychiatric hospitals are called 'Registered Mental Nurses' (RMNs) and those who work in the community are called 'Community Psychiatric Nurses' (CPNs) or 'Community Mental Health Nurses' (CMHNs). The community psychiatric nurse (CPN) is the team member who usually gives the patient any injections prescribed by the psychiatrist (although, sometimes, these are given by the general practice nurse or GP). The CPN is trained in many more aspects of mental health care than giving medication. He or she will often work as a patient's *keyworker*, which means that they are the first point of contact for the patient or their carer, and that they stay in regular contact with the patient, and are responsible for making sure that the care planned for a patient is actually delivered. The CPN is also able to refer a patient to the social services if there are 'social' problems such as worries over money (including benefits), childcare, and housing.

CPNs are trained in assessing a person's mental state and deciding, therefore, whether or not a person needs to see the psychiatrist for a review of their medication or other treatment. They may also be trained in specific treatment techniques such as relaxation therapy and the management of anxiety symptoms. Like the other team members, CPNs will spend time listening to the patient's problems and offering support, advice, and counselling.

CPNs are trained in ways of educating patients and their relatives or other carers about illnesses such as schizophrenia, which can otherwise be quite difficult to understand. They are able to advise carers about what to do when they run into difficulties.

SOCIAL WORKERS

Social workers are usually employed by the local authority (the council) and, unlike the other members of the CMHT, who are employed by NHS hospitals or community trusts, are based in social services departments. However, despite the fact that they have different employers, the different team members in a well run CMHT will meet frequently and work closely together. A social worker may also be a patient's keyworker.

The social worker is the team expert on help with social problems, including money worries, how to claim social security benefits, housing (including council housing and residential group homes), respite care, child care (such as childminding), and travel problems such as how to obtain a bus pass. Social workers may also be approved under the Mental Health Act to take part in assessing whether or not a patient should be admitted and detained compulsorily under a Section (see Chapter 6).

Social workers may be able to help with the following:

- money worries
- how to claim social security benefits
- housing, including council housing and housing in residential group homes
- respite care
- child care, such as childminding
- travel problems, such as how to obtain a bus passes

OCCUPATIONAL THERAPISTS

The special expertise of the occupational therapist, or OT, is in helping patients to develop their activities of daily living. This includes looking after themselves and their home, finding work outside the home which suits them, or perhaps finding a place on an educational or training course to improve their work skills.

The OT can arrange several daytime activities that are helpful in a person's care, may also act as a patient's keyworker, and may also offer sympathetic listening, advice, counselling, and anxiety management. The OT is not, however, unlike the community nurses, trained to give medication.

CLINICAL PSYCHOLOGISTS

Unlike psychiatrists, clinical psychologists are not medically trained and therefore cannot prescribe or advise on medication. However, like psychiatrists, they also undergo prolonged training, including a university degree, and this equips them to offer specific psychological treatments. The treatments include *cognitive therapy*, which can be most helpful for patients with depression, *anxiety management*, including relaxation exercises, and treatments for phobias. Sometimes *group or family therapy* may be offered to help patients improve their relationships with other people — including their family or other carers. Some psychologists run groups for families and other carers, which provide an opportunity to discuss worries with others who know what it is like to look after a person with schizophrenia. Unfortunately, there are not very many of these groups provided by the NHS at the moment.

Clinical psychologists are less frequently involved in the care of people with schizophrenia than the other members of the CMHT, but they may also act as keyworkers for the patient.

Crisis teams

In some parts of the country, another type of mental health team in the community is available to deal with crises. Such teams are known variously as the *Crisis Response Service, Crisis Intevention Team* or *Mental Health Rapid Response Team*. They usually consists of CPNs and social workers who are on-call out-of-hours to deal with emergencies, for example, when patients' problems suddenly worsen out-of-hours. The idea is that they can provide rapid treatment and support to patients within their own homes and thus avoid the need for hospital admission. Sometimes, such teams are made up of the same people who work in the daytime CMHT.

Counsellors

In recent years, there has been a big increase in the number of counsellors employed by GPs to help their general practice patients with emotional problems. Counsellors vary in their experience and qualifications, but should usually be accredited or approved by the British Association of Counselling (BAC).

WHAT IS COUNSELLING?

Counselling is a poorly understood term. Although the word literally means 'giving advice', mental health counselling has developed in such a way that it usually now involves listening sympathetically, and not giving direct advice at all. Mental health counsellors listen to a person with emotional problems, and then reflect what they feel are the main priorities back. The person with emotional problems is then able to start tackling the problems themself.

Although counsellors are sometimes involved in the care of a person with schizophrenia, their special expertise lies in listening and helping an individual to help themselves. This approach is not usually effective in schizophrenics who are seriously ill and suffering from hallucinations and delusions; largely because it relies on patients' insight into their own problems. One of the characteristics of schizophrenia is that people do not often recognise that they need help.

Since counsellors are not usually trained doctors or nurses, they do not usually advise on medication. And while they should be in regular contact with their client's (the patient's) GP, they will not usually meet other members of the CMHT.

───── The Care Programme Approach

In the old days, all the services and facilities needed for the care of someone with a serious mental health problem like schizophrenia were under one roof, that of the large mental hospital. Now that most people with such problems live outside hospital, however, and community services (ie, health services, social services, social security and housing) are all managed separately, there is a risk that they won't get all the care they need. The Care Programme Approach, or CPA, was introduced in 1991 to overcome this problem and ensure that the different community services are coordinated and work together towards a particular person's care. This approach requires that professionals from the health authority and local authority get together to arrange care, and applies to all patients accepted for care by the specialist mental health services.

The CPA initially requires that a professional meets with the patient and carries out an *assessment of need*. It then requires that a care plan, which addresses both a person's social, medical and nursing needs, is drawn up and written down. The different professionals involved may meet to plan the patient's care. If so, the patient, and, if they wish it, their family or other carers, will be invited to attend. These *care-planning meetings* commonly take place before the patient is discharged from hospital.

To ensure that the resultant plan is followed, one professional, often a CPN or OT (occupational therapist), but sometimes a psychiatrist or psychologist, is appointed as the patient's keyworker. The keyworker is the professional who remains in regular contact with both the patient and their carer(s) and reviews the care plan at intervals, both to ensure that it is being carried out, and to make changes to it when necessary. The keyworker has to send a copy of the patient's (written) care plan to all the professionals involved in that patient's care, including their GP. Usually — but only if the patient agrees, since it is confidential information — the keyworker will also give a copy of the care plan to the relatives or other carers.

The Care Programme Approach involves:

- Assessment of a person's health and social needs
- A care-planning meeting to which family or other carers should be invited
- The appointment of the patient's keyworker (the first contact point for both patient and carer)

───── CARE MANAGEMENT

Care management refers to the process through which social service departments try to ensure that the clients referred to them are assessed for social problems and have their problems addressed. A social service care manager usually has several clients to purchase care for and arranges for services to be provided, but does not usually provide them themselves. Care management and the CPA should work hand-in-hand to provide a patient's social and medical needs, and this will require health and social service professionals to meet at intervals to discuss patients' care.

SUPERVISION REGISTERS

Supervision registers were introduced in April 1994 to identify those people with severe mental illnesses, such as schizophrenia, who may be a significant risk to themselves or others, and to ensure that local services focus effectively on these patients, who have the greatest need of care and active follow-up. The local mental health service is responsible for taking steps to trace people on the supervision register who lose contact with services.

Whether or not a patient should be on the supervision register is decided during that patient's CPA planning meeting, usually before their discharge from hospital. During the care planning meeting, the patient will be told what information about them will be kept on the supervision register, who else will know about their placement on the register (their GP, for example) and why those people need to know.

Patients likely to be put on the supervision register are those who:

- misuse alcohol or drugs
- lack a supportive relationship (no family or close friends)
- lack suitable accommodation
- are at risk to themselves or others
- stop taking their medication

In order to meet the requirements of the supervision register, services will have to be preferentially targeted towards those patients who are most likely to fall out of contact and become lost to follow-up by the mental health team.

The Patient's Charter

The Patient's Charter was drawn up in 1991 to help improve services by informing people of their rights to health care, and of the standards they should expect the NHS to meet. Copies of the Charter are available from hospitals, GP surgeries, chemists, and Community Health Councils.

- The Charter includes standards of access to GP services, hospitals, and community services. It spells out a person's rights to health care, including: medication when necessary, to be registered with a GP, to be referred to a specialist when that GP thinks it is necessary, to have their treatment explained, and to confidentiality

PATIENT ACCESS TO OWN MEDICAL RECORDS

The Patient's Charter states that a person has the right to look at their own medical and other health records. However, in practice, this is at the discretion of the doctors involved in that person's care and, sometimes, part of the medical record may be withheld. This is usually because the doctors consider that the patient may be harmed or seriously upset by reading something about themselves in the record, but may also be because they think that the patient lacks insight into their problem and that access to the record could therefore lead to conflict and argument, damaging the patient's care.

INVOLVING RELATIVES AND FRIENDS

The Charter states that, if a patient agrees — all patients have a right to confidentiality — they can expect their relatives and friends to be kept up to date with the progress of their treatment. The keyworker will usually be responsible for keeping relatives and friends up to date with a patient's progress.

THE CHARTER AND GP SERVICES

The Charter makes it very clear that everyone has the right to be registered with a GP (the Primary Care Authority must find a doctor for you within two days), the right to a health check on joining a practice, and the right to additional health checks every three years on request. Patients on income support, family credit, or disability benefits, as well as people over sixty, are entitled to free prescriptions.

The Charter also states that GPs should provide leaflets about their services, covering all the arrangements listed in this Chapter.

THE CHARTER AND HOSPITAL SERVICES

The Charter states that nine out of 10 people can expect to be seen in the hospital outpatient clinic within 13 weeks of being referred to a specialist (a psychiatrist) by their GP. In practice, 13 weeks is a very long time for a person suffering from the more severe symptoms of schizophrenia to have to wait, and, in most parts of the country, patients are seen much more quickly — within a week or two if they are seriously ill, and on the same day if they are at immediate risk of harming themselves or others.

The Charter also states that patients can expect to be given a specific appointment time, and to be seen in the outpatient clinic within 30 minutes of that time. In practice, however, patients may have to wait longer, if, for example, the psychiatrist or CPN is called out to see another patient in an emergency.

The Charter states that patients who are admitted to hospital through the casualty (Accident & Emergency) department can expect to be found a hospital bed within four hours of admission. Unfortunately, at the time of writing, the current cut-backs and experience suggest that this target is by no means consistently achievable in these days of reduced bed numbers in psychiatric hospital wards.

Patients who are admitted to mixed wards of both men and women patients should be told in advance, and washing and toilet facilities should always be 'single-sex'.

——————— THE CHARTER AND COMMUNITY SERVICES

The Charter states that you can expect the mental health nurse (CPN) to visit a patient:

- within four hours (in the daytime), if the person has been referred to the nurse as an urgent patient
- within two working days, if the person has been referred as a non-urgent patient, and
- by appointment on the day you ask for, if you give the nurse more than 48 hours' notice.

In practice, it may not always be possible for the CPN to come on the day you ask for, because most CPNs look after about 40 patients each, all of whom must be seen on a regular basis.

How to complain

If you feel that something has gone wrong with a person's care, there are well established procedures for dealing with your complaint.

> ■ If you have a complaint about your GP, the first person to contact is that GP's practice manager

The practice manager will discuss the problem with the GP concerned and give you a response to your complaint — usually within a few days, unless the GP is away on holiday. You may then be invited to meet the GP concerned to discuss the complaint in more detail.

> ■ If you cannot sort the problem out with your own GP and practice manager, the next step is to contact your Primary Care Authority (PCA), which is the new name for the Family Health Service Authority (FHSA)

The PCA's telephone number is on your medical card, and in the telephone directory, and can also be obtained from your GP's practice. The PCA should acknowledge your complaint within two days, and sort out less serious complaints within a month. More serious complaints, such as those alleging a failure to provide proper medical care or those alleging professional misconduct, may take six months to deal with, and will usually involve a hearing to which the patient and their family or other carers will be invited.

- Complaints about treatment or care in hospital should be addressed to the hospital General Manager or Chief Executive — ward staff will tell patients and carers who this is

You can expect a response acknowledging your hospital care-related complaint within a few days. A written reply should, eventually, fully address your complaint.

- Your local *Community Health Council* is an independent source of help and advice on how to complain

The Community Health Council's number is also in the telephone book, and available from your local GP or Hospital.

- If you are still not satisfied with the responses to your complaints from the PCA or hospital, you can ask the *Health Service Commissioner for England*, also known as the *Ombudsman*, to consider investigating your complaint further

The Commissioner's contact details are:
Health Service Commissioner for England
Mill Bank Tower
Mill Bank
London SW1P 4QP
0845 015 4033

- Another source of help and advice is *Health Information First,* contactable on freephone 0800 665 544

6 Mental Health Act legislation

Individual freedom versus making sure people get the treatment they need

Some might argue that it is wrong to put people in hospital and treat them against their will — that this takes away their basic human right to freedom. On the other hand, people suffering from schizophrenia sometimes don't realise that they are ill and need help and this *'loss of insight'* may prevent them from getting the help they need. In this light, the Mental Health Act can be seen as society's way of making sure that mentally ill people get the treatment necessary to ease their problems, even when they can't see the need for it themselves. The right to receive treatment for illness is, after all, another basic human right.

The background to British mental health care

Hundreds of years ago people with mental illness were often feared, abandoned and left to fend for themselves. But, as early as the 13th century, the Bethlehem Hospital in London was founded for sufferers of mental illness. Because very little treatment existed in those days, hospitals could offer little more than asylum (which really means 'safety' or 'refuge') and this is why institutions for the mentally ill became known, in general, as mental asylums. Some, like the York Retreat set up in the 18th century, provided a good standard of care, while others became overcrowded and unable to cope. This led to some highly restrictive practices such as keeping people in hospital indefinitely and even chaining some up. Fortunately, this kind of practice ended nearly 200 years ago (after the government passed laws to ensure better provision for mental health), but things were still far from perfect.

In fact, throughout this century, large mental institutions have been criticized for the limited lifestyles they imposed on patients. Today, most such big old buildings have been closed down and people with severe mental health problems are cared for in the community instead. When their condition worsens, they are usually admitted to smaller and more 'user-friendly' units, often attached to general hospitals. However, there are times when patients may be unaware that they are becoming ill again and for this reason, mental health legislation is designed both to make sure that everyone has access to treatment and that the rights to freedom of the individual are protected. In England and Wales, mental health law is laid down in the 1983 Mental Health Act, described below. New legislation is currently being prepared. In Scotland, the equivalent is the Mental Health (Scotland) Act, 1984, and in Northern Ireland, it is the Mental Health Order (NI), 1986.

The 1983 Mental Health Act

The 1983 Mental Health Act is divided into a number of 'sections' that cover different situations relating to mental health (you may have heard doctors or social workers using the term '*to section*' someone, which means using the 1983 Act to ensure that a person goes to hospital for care). Before describing the various sections in detail, the following terms and concepts need to be explained:

MEDICAL RECOMMENDATION Contrary to popular belief, it is not actually the doctor who 'detains' a patient in hospital (this unfortunate task falls to hospital managers). Rather, doctors can only make a 'medical recommendation' that a patient be admitted

APPLICATION Once a doctor has filled out a medical recommendation form, it is then up to an approved social worker (ASW) to decide whether or not they should act on that recommendation. If they decide that they should, it is then their duty to make an 'application' to the hospital manager in question to compulsorily admit the patient

SECTION 12 APPROVED DOCTOR A 'section 12 approved' doctor is a doctor who is approved under section 12 of the Mental Health Act 1983 as having special expertise in the management of mental health problems. Most psychiatrists and certain GPs are section 12 approved, and this allows them to assess patients with a view to making a medical recommendation for admission to hospital where appropriate. Doctors have to go on training courses every few years in order to stay section 12 approved

APPROVED SOCIAL WORKER Rather like the approved doctors, social workers need to be approved under the Mental Health Act in order to assess patients with a view to acting on medical recommendations for hospital treatment. 'Approved social workers' also have to demonstrate special expertise in dealing with people who suffer from mental health problems

NEAREST RELATIVE The 'nearest relative' is usually consulted at the time a patient is being assessed for compulsory admission ('sectioned'), as the views of the family are considered very important in determining the best way to manage a patient experiencing difficulties. In law, the nearest relative is able to sign an application for the compulsory admission of a patient but, in reality, this rarely happens because it can create problems with family relationships; it is usually the ASW who makes the application instead. The term 'nearest relative' is applied to the closest competent person to the patient, who must be resident in the UK and over the age of 18

────── SECTION 136, MENTALLY DISORDERED PERSONS FOUND IN PUBLIC PLACES

Section 136:

- is applied by police officers
- to persons thought to have mental health problems
- moving them from a public place to a place of safety
- it may last up to 72 hours

The outcome may be:

- immediate discharge
- voluntary admission to hospital
- compulsory admission to hospital

────── SECTION 2, ADMISSION FOR ASSESSMENT

Section 2:

- is for the assessment of mental health problems
- needs two doctors and an approved social worker (or nearest relative)
- can last up to 28 days
- may be appealed against within 14 days

The outcome may be:

- discharge from hospital
- continued formal admission (under section 3)
- continued informal admission

Essentially, section 2 allows for the assessment of a patient who is thought to be suffering from some kind of mental disorder. The purpose of this period of assessment is to give the mental health staff time to decide what is wrong with the patient (ie, provide a diagnosis) and to form a plan of treatment if one is needed. At the end of this assessment period, a decision is made as to how best to care for the individual if mental health care is required.

────── SECTION 3, ADMISSION FOR TREATMENT

Section 3:

- is to provide treatment for mental health problems
- needs two doctors and an approved social worker (or nearest relative)
- can last up to six months
- may be appealed against in the first six months

The outcome may be:

- discharge from hospital
- continued formal admission (under section 3), renewed for 6 months and then 12 months
- continued informal admission

The main difference between sections 2 and 3 is that section 2 is for a brief period of assessment while section 3 is for a longer period of treatment. In applying for section 2, the mental health staff are seeking an opportunity to decide exactly what is wrong with the patient. Under section 3, since the patient is already known to the mental health services and it is assumed that there is an existing diagnosis, there is no need to repeat compulsory assessment, and a period of treatment can begin immediately. For this reason, section 3 is sometimes known as a 'treatment order'. In Scotland, the equivalent of section 3 is covered by Section 18 of the Mental Health (Scotland) Act, 1984.

SECTION 4, EMERGENCY ADMISSION FOR ASSESSMENT

Section 4:
- is for emergencies only (eg, where only the GP is available)
- needs one doctor and an ASW to apply it
- can last up to 72 hours
- usually leads to section 2 for formal assessment

Section 4 is covered in Scotland by section 24 of the Mental Health (Scotland) Act, 1984.

SECTION 5 (2)

This applies to the detention of a patient already in hospital who wishes to leave against the hospital doctor's advice. It is a temporary order applied by the hospital doctor and lasts for up to 72 hours. After this time, the patient may leave, unless section 2 or 3 has been applied in the interim.

SECTION 5 (4)

This is a temporary holding order similar to section 5 (2), but applied by a senior hospital nurse and lasting for only up to six hours, unless another section is applied in the interim.

In Scotland, section 25(2) allows a fully qualified nurse to detain an informal patient for up to two hours or until the (earlier) arrival of a doctor, if it seems that this might benefit the patient's own health or safety, or help protect others. The two-hour period cannot be extended. Similarly, in Ireland, a nurse may hold a patient for the same reasons, but for no more than six hours, or until the (earlier) arrival of a doctor.

SECTIONS 35, 36, 37, 38, AND 41

Any of these sections may be applied by the Crown or Magistrates' Courts, if they decide that a person who has been arrested by the police ought to be detained in a hospital, for the care or treatment of mental illness, rather than a prison. In each case, the person detained should given written information about the section of the Mental Health Act under which they are being held, and about how they may appeal against it.

Compulsory treatment

In all cases, the psychiatrist must first offer treatment to the patient directly and ask for his or her consent to it. If that consent is not given, but the psychiatrist believes the treatment in question to be essential to the patient's wellbeing, then sections 2 and 3 of the Mental Health Act allow the psychiatrist to treat the patient with medication for up to three months without the patient's consent. (This clause applies to medication only; treatment with electroconvulsive therapy (ECT) may only be given without the patient's consent after a second opinion from another consultant psychiatrist.)

After three months, if further treatment with medication is needed, the psychiatrist must again ask for the patient's consent. If the patient still fails to give consent (and the psychiatrist considers the treatment essential), the psychiatrist must arrange for a second opinion from another consultant psychiatrist. Furthermore, the appointment of this second psychiatrist is the job of an independent body, the Mental Health Act Commission.

THE MENTAL HEALTH ACT COMMISSION

The *Mental Health Act Commission* is a public body or special health authority made up of doctors, social workers, nurses, psychologists, lawyers, and lay-people. It is responsible to the government for drawing up a code of practice for the Mental Health Act and for overseeing the facilities provided for detained patients. The Commission carries out official visits to hospitals and may interview detained patients and their relatives and hear any complaints they have. Its address and telephone number is:

Mental Health Act Commission
Maid Marian House
56 Hounds Gate
Nottingham NGI 6BG
Tel: 0115 943 7100

Appealing against being held in hospital

The Mental Health Act Commission does not have the power to release detained patients.

> ■ If a patient or their nearest relative disagrees with a detainment order, they may appeal either to the *Mental Health Review Tribunal* (MHRT), or to *'hospital managers'*

Very soon after being admitted to hospital under a section of the Mental Health Act, patients should be given written information (usually leaflets) about their rights while in hospital and about the ways in which they may appeal. In Scotland, appeals can be made either to the Sheriff's court or the Mental Welfare Commission for Scotland, at K Floor, Argyle House, 3 Lady Lawson Street, Edinburgh EH3 9SH, Tel: 0131 222 6111.

The Mental Health Review Tribunal (MHRT) is an independent organization set up by the government to act like a 'mobile court'. It comprises a lawyer, a doctor (independent of the hospital) and a lay member, all three of whom must come from outside the hospital. The lawyer, or solicitor, may be paid for through *Legal Aid* which, since April 1994, has been available to all patients attending MHRTs, whatever their income. The Law Society publishes a list of solicitors approved to act in MHRT cases, available from:

> The Law Society
> Ipsley Court
> Berrington Close
> Redditch
> Worcestershire B98 0TD
> Tel: 0171 242 1222

Any patient formally admitted for assessment under section 2 has the right to appeal against compulsory admission, and may do so within the first 14 days of the 28-day period. Patients admitted under section 3 need to appeal within the first six months of their detainment.

Appeals are made to the MHRT, which then has a duty to meet with both the patient and those involved in the patient's care, to decide whether or not formal detainment is still necessary. The MHRT listens to the views of the patient, the patient's doctor and other caring professionals. It then decides whether to discharge the patient from the section or to uphold it. Alternatively, the patient may be allowed a period of leave away from the hospital, or be transferred to another hospital. In some cases, the patient may be discharged from the section but remain in hospital for a while on an informal, ie, voluntary, basis.

The addresses of the regional MHRT offices are:

South East Mental Health Review Tribunal
Block 3, Crown Offices
Kingston Bypass
Surbiton
Surrey KT6 5QN
Tel: 0208 268 4520

London North Mental Health Review Tribunal
Block I, Spur 3, Canon's Park Government Buildings
Honeypot Lane
Stanmore
Middlesex HA7 1AY
Tel: 0207 972 3734

North West/East Mental Health Review Tribunal
3rd Floor, Cressington House
249 St Mary's Road
Garston
Liverpool
Merseyside LI9 0NF
Tel: 0151 494 0095

Midlands Mental Health Review Tribunal
Spur A, Block 5, Government Buildings
Chalfont Drive
Western Boulevard
Nottingham NG8 3RZ
Tel: 0115 929 4222

Northern Ireland Mental Health Review Tribunal
Room 105, Dundonald House
Upper Newtonards Road
Belfast BT4 3SF
01232 485 550

Wales Mental Health Review Tribunal
Ist Floor, New Crown Buildings
Cathay's Park
Cardiff CF1 3NQ
Tel: 02920 825 328

HOSPITAL MANAGERS

The hospital managers involved in appeals against detention are not the paid managers who work in the NHS, but lay people appointed by the local health authority (much like school governors) — usually members of the local community with an interest in the welfare of people who suffer from mental health problems. Hospital managers are obliged to refer any patient who has been detained under section 3 for six months and who has not applied to a MHRT themselves, to an MHRT.

Legislation concerned with Care in the Community

The sections described above are all concerned with detention in hospital. In these days of provision of *Care in the Community*, the law has been developed to apply to some patients after they leave hospital too.

─── SECTION 117, AFTERCARE

■ Section 117 requires the Local Health Authority and Local Authority Social Services between them to provide care for all people discharged from a section 3 detainment, until they are satisfied that such care is no longer necessary

A section 117 care plan may include advising the patient as to where they might live (perhaps in an aftercare hostel or group home, rather than on their own) and how often they should see their keyworker. Patients usually have to consent to their aftercare plan before they are allowed to leave hospital.

─── SUPERVISED DISCHARGE

Since April 1996, under the Mental Health (Patients in the Community) Act, supervised discharge has been introduced for certain patients previously detained under the Mental Health Act, 1983.

■ Supervised discharge is designed to help those patients who go through repeated cycles of admission to hospital, improvement, release, breakdown in arrangements for their care in the community, failed community care, and rapid readmission to hospital

This pattern tends to recur because certain people stop taking their medication and drop out of contact with their keyworker. These unfortunates have earnt the nickname 'revolving door patients'.

A patient subject to supervised discharge must abide by the care plan drawn up for them before they leave hospital, at their section 117 meeting. A supervisor, who will, in most cases, also be the patient's keyworker, is appointed at this meeting and given the power to:

- ensure that the patient lives in a specified place
- ensure that the patient attends for medical treatment
- take the patient to the place where they are supposed to attend for medical treatment.

─── GUARDIANSHIP

In Scotland and Northern Ireland, a patient over 16 years of age may be 'received into guardianship'. This requires an application similar to the 518 application for admission.

In Northern Ireland the application for guardianship must be supported by two medical recommendations and one from a social worker. The guardian (who will be either the local authority or a person chosen or accepted by the local authority) must be named and is then given the powers to specify where the patient will live, where he or she will go for treatment, what his or her occupation, education or training should be, and to enforce that access is given to a doctor, MHO or other similar person.

Proposed changes in the Mental Health Law

In 1998 the government Department of Health (DoH) began looking at ways to improve mental health legislation. It was felt that the existing system was rather cumbersome and time-consuming to manage and that things could be improved for everyone concerned if the law were changed. With this in mind the Department of Health (DoH) has set up the *Scoping Study Committee* whose task it is to undertake a radical review of the Mental Health Act.

At the time of writing (June 1999), their proposals for the new legislation do seem to differ quite radically from the existing legislation, and also seem to be more streamlined for both patients and professionals. An outline of the proposed changes is given below.

WORKING TOGETHER

In the past, people with mental health problems have sometimes seemed to 'fall between two stools', namely the Health and Social Services. Sometimes they have been 'lost to follow-up', for example through a change of address, and in rare instances this has led to disastrous consequences, including homicide. Inquiries have suggested that one of the causative problems has been a lack of communication between the various agencies providing care and, in an effort to overcome this, the Scoping Committee is considering recommending the introduction of a statutory duty on all relevant agencies to work together. The term they use for working together is *reciprocity*.

FORMAL ASSESSMENT

The power to assess those deemed in need of mental health care regardless of whether or not they comply has been recommended. Like the existing sections, this would be a time-limited power. The assessment might take place in a hospital or community setting, but, unless the patient agrees to it, or the case is deemed an emergency, treatment should not be provided. The assessment should be approved by at least two approved professionals, one of whom should be a medical practitioner. The assessment should cover: capacity, risk, diagnosis, and formulation of and agreement on care and treatment plans. At the end of the assessment period, if enforced treatment is recommended, the clinical team should submit to an independent tribunal.

———— THE TRIBUNAL

The establishment of an *independent specialist tribunal*, appointed by the Lord Chancellor's Department, has also been recommended. This tribunal would make decisions on all applications for *compulsion* (the enforcing of assessment, treatment or detainment). It would replace, completely, all the Mental Health Review Tribunals and would comprise a senior lawyer, a medical practitioner and someone with knowledge of social care provision, all of whom would have received appropriate training.

The proposed role of the new tribunal

- To determine whether compulsion is appropriate in terms of the diagnosis, the capacity (patient's ability to make important decisions) and the risk. If yes:
- To determine site and type of compulsion (eg, hospital or community setting)
- To approve the compulsive care and treatment plan
- To (once the patient is ready) approve discharge from compulsive treatment

The tribunal would have the power to issue compulsory orders that lasted for up to six months. Patients would be able to appeal to the tribunal against those orders that exceeded three months and the tribunal would have the power of discharge (it is interesting to note that patients would appeal to the same body that issued the treatment order in the first place). Similarly, the tribunal would be able to order renewals on the recommendation of the clinical supervisor. The clinical supervisor would have the power to discharge a patient subject to an order, but only with the tribunal's approval.

———— TREATMENT

The Scoping Study Committee would prefer to leave the term 'treatment' undefined. However, they specify those types of treatment that require special *safeguards* and state that the safeguards should be defined in the legislation. These treatments include:

- Neurosurgery for mental disorder (brain surgery)
- Electroconvulsive therapy (ECT)
- Longer periods of medication
- Depot medication, polypharmacy and doses above the levels recommended (in the 'British National Formulary')
- Feeding against the will of the patient
- Treatment for physical injury arising as a consequence of mental disorder

The need, in certain situations, to administer emergency treatment is recognized. The

Committee states that all emergency treatment should be reported to the tribunal when a patient's case is next under discussion.

POSITIVE RIGHTS

The Committee recommends the inclusion of a number of patient 'rights' in the legislation. These include the right (in certain circumstances) to an assessment, the right to information about treatment and care, the right to independent legal advice, the right to an 'authorized representative' and the right to an adequate level of services, including ongoing care after compulsion.

CAPACITY AND INFORMAL DETENTION

Capacity is a legal term that refers to someone's ability (capacity) to make important decisions, generally about their own life. In terms of mental health law, capacity generally relates to decisions about care and treatment. If someone who has the capacity decides that they do not want treatment, their decision must be respected. However, someone who does not have the capacity may still receive necessary treatment under the Mental Health Act (1983), even if they decline it. Often, people without the capacity do not object to treatment, however, and the legal situation in England and Wales relating to their management has been unclear. Frequently, they are cared for informally in 'closed' settings, as if detained under a section, but a recent legal case, Bournewood, has made it clear that such 'informal detention' is no longer acceptable.

The Bournewood case

Bournewood NHS Hospital Trust was taken to court in 1997 because an informally detained patient was prevented from leaving the hospital, but not under a section of the Mental Health Act. The High Court ruled in favour of the Trust, on the basis that the patient lacked the capacity to decide whether or not they should stay in hospital. However, the case went on to the Court of Appeal, which ruled in favour of the patient, effectively stating that the patient should only have been detained under the Mental Health Act. The case then went before the highest court in the land, the House of Lords, which overruled the Appeal Court and decided in favour of the NHS Trust. At the time of writing (June 1999) the European Court in Strasbourg is hearing the case —the ruling may be reversed yet again.

PREVENTIVE DETENTION

The Government is currently considering a controversial proposal to detain certain people who are considered dangerous (ie, those with certain types of personality disorder) but who *have not yet committed* a violent act. There are an estimated 4000–5000 such people in the country. This proposal, ie, to detain individuals considered 'dangerous' before they have done anything wrong, has aroused strong feelings among human rights groups.

SAFEGUARDS

Second opinion approved doctors

Under the present system, patients under a treatment order (ie, section 3) must have their treatment reviewed after three months by an 'outside' and 'second opinion approved' doctor (SOAD). This helps to ensure that the compulsory treatment given is right for the patient concerned. Under the new recommendations, the medical member of the new tribunal will fulfil the role of second opinion approved doctor.

The Mental Health Act Commission

The Committee recommends the continuation of a body such as the MHAC but recommends that it should be independent of the Secretary of State for Health, instead reporting directly to Parliament (through the select committee structure). Its role should be expanded to include the monitoring of care of all patients under compulsion, whether in hospital or community settings. The new body should also monitor the care of informally detained hospital patients.

Nearest relative and advocates

The Committee, while recognizing the importance of the role of nominated relatives, friends or carers, is recommending the removal of the nearest relative's powers with respect to both application and discharge. The Committee also recommends arrangements to ensure the availability of trained advocacy (legal) services, and the importance of people with mental health problems having access to someone who can help them put across their needs and wishes.

Comment

The working of the new Mental Health (Patients in the Community) Act in England and Wales is subject to a written code of practice drawn up by the Mental Health Act Commission. Although it is unfortunate that laws have to be passed which in some ways restrict the freedom of people suffering from illnesses such as schizophrenia, the current legislation is a big improvement on the past — when patients could be held in hospital for long periods without the option of appealing against their restraint. Every effort is made to keep patients out of hospital, but this does mean that the doctors and social workers responsible for them in the community do sometimes need the power to insist that they continue with their care and treatment. It is unfortunate that some patients with schizophrenia turn away from help just when they need it most, but this reinforces the need for some legislation.

If patients or their families or friends have complaints about or comments on how the new laws are working, they should not feel afraid to express their views to the Mental Health Act Commission (see page 46 for contact details).

■ **Note:** The information regarding the Mental Health Acts given here is abbreviated. More specific detail on any particular case should be sought from an appropriate legal body or a specialist voluntary advice line (see Chapter 8)

■ **More information:** More information on the proposed changes in mental health legislation can be obtained from the internet simply by typing 'Mental Health Law' into a search engine such as 'Yahoo' or 'Altavista'. Another useful source of information for patients, relatives and mental health professionals, is the *Institute of Mental Health Law*, founded by the solicitor Peter Edwards — its web address is: http://www.imhl.co.uk. Yet another body, the *European Institute of Mental Health Law*, is currently being set up — its web address is: http://www.euroimhl.com/contacts.htm

7 Problems associated with schizophrenia

Most people with schizophrenia can lead stable and meaningful lives in the community. Reading the papers or listening to the news, however, you could almost be led to believe that people with schizophrenia are all unpredictable and dangerous. The reality is that most — nine out of 10 — people with schizophrenia never hurt themselves or others, but serious incidents do occasionally occur and the press is obliged to report them and this means that most people without personal experience of schizophrenia hear only about the violent or self-destructive behaviour of some sufferers.

■　Nine out of 10 people with schizophrenia do not try to hurt themselves or others

There are reasons why some people suffering from schizophrenia become desperate and consider suicide, and also reasons why some can become frightened and hostile or even violent towards others. Violence is sometimes directed at the person's family or other carers, the very people who are providing most support. Only on rare occasions is violence directed at complete strangers. Moreover, such occasions are frequently predictable and prevented by adequate care and supervision.

─── Depression and suicide

People with schizophrenia are at risk of becoming depressed, and it is usually this depression which leads some of them to try to end their lives. There is some debate among experts as to whether such depression is actually part of the schizophrenic illness, or a separate condition that results from the effects of schizophrenia. Sometimes depression seems to occur just after a patient has recovered from a schizophrenic 'breakdown', and is no longer suffering from their more severe symptoms such as hallucinations or delusions (see Chapter 1). They may have just left hospital and may well be having trouble coming to terms with the seriousness of their illness and the impact that it has had and will have on their lives. Overall, some 20% of people with schizophrenia also suffer from depression.

●　20% of people with schizophrenia suffer from depression
●　10% of people with schizophrenia commit suicide

Patients suffering from schizophrenia may also feel guilty about how they behaved when they were really ill, and that they have, in some way, let their family and friends down. They may feel anxious about developing another bout of schizophrenia, grieve for the job they lost, the qualifications they failed to get, or the girlfriend or boyfriend they lost because of their illness. All their hopes and expectations for their lives will probably have to change, and it is therefore no surprise that many develop depression.

RECOGNIZING DEPRESSION

It is not always obvious when someone is depressed. Although depressed people usually look low and unhappy, may cry, and may say how depressed they feel, this is not always the case — some people may be feeling suicidal inside, yet on the surface appear calm or even happy. To the experienced, however, an individual's behaviour will usually change in some way when they are depressed and it is therefore important for carers to try to recognise such signs in their relatives.

- Depression is a serious but treatable condition
- It is not always obvious when someone is depressed

Changes in depressed patients include changes in sleep patterns, appetite and activity level. Depressed people will almost certainly stop enjoying the things in life that used to give them pleasure, such as hobbies, sports, or seeing friends. They often neglect themselves, lose their self-esteem, and stop looking after their appearance and their home. They may become irritable and unfriendly and impatient, and put other people off helping them. Unfortunately, this type of behaviour tends to increase the person's loneliness and isolation, making them more depressed, and so on.

Changes in someone who is becoming depressed include:

- Looking miserable and unhappy, and possibly (but not always) crying
- Losing interest and enjoyment in the better things in life
- Sleeping more or sleeping less
- Appetite and weight going up or down
- Activity level going up or down — they are either unable to keep still, or have slowed right down
- Irritability and impatience — they may complain more than usual
- Loss of self-esteem, feelings of guilt, feeling unworthy of help
- Withdrawal, isolation
- Self-neglect, poor hygiene, neglect of their home
- Drinking more alcohol

Some people try to relieve their feelings of depression by drinking more alcohol than usual. This may make them feel better while they drink, but, unfortunately, is highly likely to make them more depressed once the good feeling or 'high' has worn off. In the long term, alcohol increases the risk of more serious depression, and suicide is more likely when a person is drunk. Certain illegal drugs have a similar effect.

It you suspect that the person in your care is becoming depressed, it is essential that you try to get them to see a doctor or other professional as soon as possible. While psychological support or antidepressant treatment can often help, untreated depression can worsen to the extent that the person begins to contemplate suicide.

HOW TO PREDICT SUICIDE

It is impossible to predict suicide in a given individual with absolute certainty — all the research on risk looks at populations of people at risk and not single cases. It is important that carers realise this, because, if they don't, they can, quite wrongly, feel extremely guilty that they didn't intervene when their loved one attempts or completes suicide. Essentially, suicide is not always preventable, even with the best care in the world.

Having said, that, research studies have found that suicide is more likely in some groups of people with schizophrenia than others. The risk of suicide is higher in younger patients, in men than in women, in single than in married individuals, among those who have previously experienced a suicide in their family, among those who drink a lot of alcohol or abuse drugs, and among those who have recently been discharged from hospital. It is important to realise, however, that these so-called 'risk factors' are just a guide to a possible increase in risk in a particular group of people and are not necessarily very helpful in predicting suicide in any particular case.

Moreover, even among a group of patients who had all these risk factors — ie, a group of young single men with schizophrenia who drank a lot of alcohol, had family histories of suicide, and had recently come out of hospital — the largest majority would not commit suicide.

The risk of suicide among schizophrenic patients is definitely greater if:

- the patient is depressed
- the patient has tried to commit suicide before
- the patient has recently been bereaved or suffered some other major upset or severe stress
- the patient keeps talking about ending their life
- the patient seems to have no hope for the future
- the patient suddenly makes a will
- the patient starts to write suicide notes

Some groups of patients are also generally more at risk:

- single young men
- those recently discharged from hospital
- those who drink too much alcohol, or abuse drugs
- those with a family history of suicide

Individuals who have previously tried to commit suicide are at a considerably greater risk of trying again. This is true even if the previous suicide attempt didn't seem to be very serious, or if the person seemed to know that they would be found out and, therefore, prevented from going through with it. Those who talk about killing themselves are also more at risk of going through with it, even though their talk may sometimes seem more of an idle threat, or even a means of getting their own way. People who don't talk about suicide directly, but continually state that everything is hopeless and there is no point in trying to go on are also at greater risk, as are those who have recently been bereaved or had a major upset or trauma. Individuals who suddenly write a will or start to write suicide notes must be considered very vulnerable and every effort should be made to get them to see their GP, psychiatrist, or community psychiatric nurse.

Getting help when you are worried about suicide

- If you, as the carer, are in contact with the psychiatrist or a community psychiatric nurse, it is important that you bring depression and any hint of suicide to their attention
- If you, as the carer, are in contact with the psychiatric services, it is important that the problem is brought to the attention of the patient's general practitioner

Many people who commit suicide consult their GP more frequently in the weeks leading up to their death. It seems that this is a cry for help, but, unfortunately, they do not always find it easy to let their doctor know how depressed they have become. They may feel they should put on a brave face for the world, or may be so depressed that they can't think straight and so don't get across to the doctor how bad they feel. It can be very helpful if someone who knows how they have been feeling, ie, their carer, goes to the doctor with them. It may also help to write things down, so as not to forget them when in the doctor's surgery. GPs will usually go through each point and answer each question carefully, if asked.

Most cases of depression are treatable with psychological support or antidepressant drugs. Antidepressants are not like tranquillisers (such as Valium) which sometimes just make people drowsy and can stop them thinking clearly. Antidepressants are not addictive and they can easily be stopped, once they have worked to relieve the symptoms of depression —usually after four to six months. If antidepressants are prescribed, it may be appropriate for the carer to keep the bottle of pills and give them to the sufferer under supervision, to prevent fatal overdose. But, as always, a balance does need to be struck between taking all control away from the patient and keeping them safe.

Sometimes, a patient is so desperate and so sure that they must end their life, or that they do not deserve to live, that they refuse to see a doctor or to accept that they need help. Such cases may have to be admitted compulsorily under a section of the Mental Health Act (see Chapter 6).

Violent behaviour

It cannot be emphasized enough that the vast majority of people with schizophrenia are never violent. The following information concerns those rare occasions when violence does occur.

Most violent behaviour by people with schizophrenia is unplanned and on the spur of the moment. The patient probably won't have thought through the consequences and will very likely deeply regret their behaviour afterwards. Many people behave like this at sometime in their lives — they don't have to have schizophrenia to do so.

The same factors that increase the risk of self-harm in schizophrenia can also increase the risk of violence. The violence is often directed at the people nearest them, their family, or other carers. Certain groups of people with schizophrenia are more likely to be violent, namely young single men, especially those who misuse alcohol or drugs, those who have been under severe stress, and those with a past history of violence. Needless to say, these risk factors for violent behaviour apply equally to many young men without schizophrenia in the general population, and we should remember that only a very small proportion of all violent acts are committed by people with schizo-phrenia. Anxiety and depression may themselves lead to irritability, hostility, and violence at times.

The risk of violence is increased in:

- Young, single, men
- Anxious, depressed, and irritable people
- Those who have recently undergone bad experiences or periods of severe stress
- Those who misuse alcohol or drugs
- Those with a past history of previous violence
- Those who develop delusions of persecution

That said, there is one situation which, while uncommon, is particularly dangerous in schizophrenia, and has led to tragedies including the killing of complete strangers. This is the development of a delusion, or false belief, by the person with schizophrenia that someone else is out to hurt them, control them in some way, or even kill them. Such delusions of persecution obviously only happen when some schizophrenic people are very ill and cannot see that their beliefs are false.

A dangerously violent situation could arise from the following:

- A person with schizophrenia believes someone is out to hurt them and can't be persuaded it's not true
- A person with schizophrenia says they are going to hurt another person in a particular way, and perhaps gets hold of a weapon
- A person with schizophrenia is not receiving care or supervision by the mental health services

Under a delusion of persecution, some patients with schizophrenia may strike first in the belief that they are preventing themselves from being hurt or killed by whoever they think is out to harm them. This is just one reason why it is very important to take people with schizophrenia seriously when they say that someone else is trying to control, dominate, or hurt them. With professional help, perhaps through increased drug treatment, such delusions can either be removed or at least reduced in strength to the degree that the patient is no longer 'dangerous'.

Lack of care and supervision

The most dangerous situations arise when someone with schizophrenia is experiencing delusions of persecution and is receiving no care, monitoring, or supervision by professionals. All the well publicized tragedies ending in killing have usually occurred in situations in which the patient had already lost all contact with professional help, and had no-one taking responsibility for ensuring that they received the treatment they needed. Such situations are not as easy to avoid as it might seem, of course, because, by its very nature, schizophrenia alters a person's own ability to recognise that they need help; insight into their condition is often lacking just when they need help most. The Government has introduced the Supervision Register (see Chapter 6) to try to ensure that those patients most at risk of hurting themselves or others receive extra help and supervision.

Getting help when you are worried about violent behaviour

> ■ If a person has been violent previously, while suffering from a breakdown of their schizophrenia, and they begin to show signs of behaving in a similar way — ie, possibly early signs of another breakdown, or relapse — it is essential to seek help early

Often, when the patient relapses relatively often, family or other carers begin to recognise the early warning signs. The signs might include a change in the patient's sleep pattern, anxiousness or irritability, or odd behaviour such as saying strange things or hearing voices.

> ■ It is particularly important to get more help and treatment for a person who is talking about harming someone else, particularly if they seem to be planning some specific action or are gathering weapons to use

Risk should be assessed by a professional, preferably a psychiatrist or CPN. If the patient is in contact with the psychiatric services, his or her family or other carers should have the telephone number of the keyworker assigned under the Care Programme Approach (see Chapter 6). The keyworker is the first line of contact. Otherwise, it is the GP. If the patient does not have a keyworker, is not registered with a GP, is not known to the mental health services, and either refuses to go and sign on with a doctor, or go to hospital, then the police may have to become involved. Someone must take responsibility for ensuring that action is taken. Sometimes the person's family or other carers might have to keep insisting that a doctor or other professional assesses the person and the risk of violence. It is vital that the assessing professionals have all the information that the carers can provide them with.

Dealing with danger

■ If a situation makes you feel frightened it is likely to be a dangerous situation. Do not dismiss your feelings

When actually faced with violent behaviour it helps, if you can, to remain as calm as possible. Try not to react by shouting back or hitting back at the violent person. Sympathise with the way they feel, but tell them that their behaviour is frightening you, and leave as soon as possible. Try to avoid being trapped — keep between the violent person and the door so that you can get out. Don't take any chances, and leave sooner rather than later, particularly if there are young children in the house where someone is being aggressive or violent.

How to handle a dangerous situation:

- Remain as calm as possible
- Try not to react by shouting back or hitting back
- Sympathise with the way the patient is feeling — even if you don't understand it
- Tell them that their behaviour is frightening you
- Leave as soon as possible
- Try to avoid being trapped
- Try to keep between the violent person and the door so that you can get out
- Don't take any chances
- Leave sooner rather than later

How to help someone who does not want treatment

It is difficult to help someone who refuses to accept that they need treatment and won't see a doctor or nurse or social worker or other professional. However, something can often be done. The person might accept treatment from their own GP, for example, especially if they have already known that GP for some years. The GP might then be able to start treatment directly, having discussed the patient's case with a psychiatrist over the telephone. The person might better accept treatment and the fact that they are mentally ill, if the words 'schizophrenia', 'psychosis', and even 'mental illness', are avoided. Instead, they could be asked to accept drug treatment on the basis that it would help them to sleep and feel calmer.

If the patient poses no risk to themselves or others, and their health is not deteriorating to the point where they are neglecting themselves, it is reasonable to wait and then try repeatedly, but gently, to get them to see the relevant doctor. Moreover, it is also essential to avoid pressurizing patients and certainly not a good idea to try to trick them into seeing a psychiatrist — they will become suspicious of any further attempts to help them. Conversely, if the patient seems to be seriously suicidal, or their behaviour poses a threat to others, and they refuse to seek help, they may have to be admitted to hospital compulsorily under a section of the Mental Health Act (see Chapter 6). Sectioning should only be used when really necessary. In an ideal world, in which adequate services were provided in hospitals and the community, every person suffering from schizophrenia should be able to get the treatment they need.

SECTION 13

Section 13 of The Mental Health Act (1983) provides for the assessment in the community of someone with mental health problems, at the request of a carer or nearest relative. Therefore, if a carer is concerned that their loved one needs medical attention but is unwilling to accept it, the carer can contact the local social services department and request a mental health assessment under section 13. The social services are then obliged to try and arrange a suitable assessment (usually with the patient's GP).

8   Helping carers

Carers' groups and support networks

Those who care for relatives or friends with schizophrenia are not alone. In many parts of the country, carers have come together to form groups which meet from time to time to give each other support, advice, and information. There may be a group like this already in existence in your district. If so, the CPN, social worker, psychiatrist, or GP should be able to put you in touch. If there is no such group in your area, and you feel energetic enough and can enlist the help of other carers, you might even consider starting one up.

Support, advice, and information

Carers' groups usually aim to support and inform their members, and allow them to share advice and experiences. Support may take the form of sympathy and encouragement expressed during a group meeting, or of a one-to-one conversation with another carer who has been through similar experiences. Advice from other carers is often extremely valuable, as they will have 'been there' themselves. Some groups arrange for some members to remain available to others for telephone calls relating to problems with schizophrenia late into the night.

The information provided might include details of day centres, employment schemes, accommodation, and respite care. Much of it will be 'word of mouth' — the more experienced carers can quickly pass on information to the less experienced.

Helping your sufferer to stay well

Carers can best help themselves by helping their relatives or friends with schizophrenia to stay well. To remind you, this can best be done in the following ways:

ENCOURAGING THE PATIENT TO TAKE THEIR MEDICATION

The chances of schizophrenia worsening, or another severe episode (a 'relapse') occurring, are more than halved in most cases if the patient continues to take long-term medication. Their carer(s) may be best placed to make sure the person actually takes the medication, because occasional side-effects, such as drowsiness, odd movement difficulties, restlessness, and other effects (see Chapter 3) may put the patient off. In such circumstances, it is important to consult the GP, CPN, or psychiatrist, since there are usually things that can be done to relieve side-effects without stopping drug treatment entirely. Stopping medication may well cause a relapse.

> ■ Medication should never be stopped without consulting the doctor

AVOIDING CRITICISM AND OVER-INVOLVEMENT

As discussed in Chapter 2, people with schizophrenia often need space and time alone, and may find it hard to play a full role in family life. Criticizing them for 'laziness', or trying too hard to get them to take part, may actually pressurise them and increase the risk of relapse. It is best to avoid too much 'expressed emotion' (see Chapter 2), including not just critical comments, but over-protectiveness and 'smothering', and expectations of frequent physical contact should be lowered.

> ■ Avoid too much expressed emotion

STAYING SANE YOURSELF

It's very important for anybody faced with caring for a person with schizophrenia to look after themselves too, as their job may go on for some years. Giving yourself time and space is important and enough rest will help to guard against your own exhaustion and depression, and against becoming unsympathetic towards your loved one. Ideally, several hours each week should be taken as a *respite break* from caring, and all carers should give themselves one or two weeks off, as a block, a year.

We all, including schizophrenia sufferers, have to live within the limits of tolerance of those around us, so it is quite acceptable for you, the carer, to occasionally say 'no'. Some schizophrenia-related behaviour may well be intolerable, and limits will need to be set, with help from the CPN, social worker, or doctor. Day centres and day hospitals should be provided in every district and if they are not, it may be necessary for carers to campaign for them — another useful function of carers' groups.

Finally, it is essential to remember that, if you have a son or daughter with schizophrenia, whatever caused it, it is not your fault!

'Staying sane' checklist

- Give yourself space and time to relax
- Find out about respite care, on a weekly basis as well as for holiday cover
- Learn to say no when necessary
- Seek professional help in setting limits on difficult behaviour
- Remember — the illness is not your fault!

Voluntary organizations that can help

Voluntary organizations that can help include MIND, The National Schizophrenia Fellowship, Voices, SANE and the Samaritans.

MIND

MIND, the national association for mental health, was set up in 1946. It is a charitable organization run by volunteers (many of them carers or ex-carers of people with schizophrenia) and funded mainly by donations, subscriptions, charity shops, and sponsored events. MIND campaigns for a better life for people diagnosed, 'labelled', or treated as mentally ill, and for their right to lead an active and valued life in the community. The organization pushes for the rights of sufferers and, therefore, sometimes finds itself in opposition to doctors and other professional
groups — over issues such as electroconvulsive therapy (ECT), for example, which some people strongly object to. MIND especially stresses the needs of black people, women, and other groups it regards as particularly vulnerable or oppressed.

MIND can help carers by putting them in touch with a network of supporters throughout England and Wales.

MIND services include:

Relatives' support schemes	Legal help
Counselling	Education
Crisis helplines	Publishing
Employment projects	Mental health bookshops
Training schemes	Special needs housing
Drop-in centres	Day centres
Befriending	Advocacy

Legal help from MIND includes advice and guidance from a network of more than 600 lawyers in England and Wales. The organization has represented both sufferers and carers in court, in some selected test cases.

Educational activities arranged by MIND include courses, workshops, and conferences. (A workshop is a group meeting in which the group members address specific tasks rather than simply having a speaker talk to them.) MIND publishes books and leaflets on mental illness and its treatment, legal issues, benefits and employment, community care, racial and gender issues, the special problems of young people, making wills, and dealing with death.

For information on publications, contact MIND publications on 0208 221 9666. For general information, contact MIND on its info-line, 0345 660 163 (local rates charged), or 0208 522 1728 (in London).

MIND has regional offices in the north, north-west, south-east, south-west, West Midlands, Trent & Yorkshire and Wales. The address of the national office is:

> MIND
> Granta House
> 15-19 Broadway
> Stratford
> London E15 4BQ

THE NATIONAL SCHIZOPHRENIA FELLOWSHIP (NSF)

The NSF was founded by a carer, John Pringle, in 1972. It is a national organization for all matters concerning people with experience of schizophrenia, including families, carers, and dependents. It comprises a network of more than 160 local community self-help groups, all made up of carers.

The NSF is a charity, funded by grants and donations, fundraising activities, members' subscriptions, and local authority (council) and health authority contracts for services performed.

NSF services include:

Housing projects	Day care projects
Befriending	Family support
Training courses for professionals	Expert conferences
Advice and information	Holidays
Quarterly members' newsletter	Books and leaflets

The NSF is currently asking for the current programme of hospital closures to be slowed right down until more community services can be provided to take the place of the hospitals being closed. It wants more social workers and CPNs trained, and more small, domestic-style, community homes built.

The NSF provides advice on the care and treatment of schizophrenia, hospital admissions, welfare benefits, how to make or change a will or a covenant, available accommodation, family problems, and holiday breaks. It runs one-day training courses for social workers, community psychiatric nurses, the police, the probation service, psychiatrists, and GPs. Books and leaflets on schizophrenia available from the NSF discuss the illness, its symptoms, treatment, and the provision of care and support services, with titles such as: *Care and aftercare, Cognitive therapy, Disability living allowance, Finding the right medication, Sulpiride, Risperidone, Clozapine, Notes on wills and trusts, Psychiatric diagnosis, Silent partners — the needs and experiences of people who care for people with a severe mental illness, Sudden death, What is schizophrenia?*

> ■ The NSF advice line is 0181 974 6814, and open from Monday to Friday between 10 am and 3 pm

The NSF has regional offices in central London, Southampton, West Bromwich, Bridgend, Exeter, Belfast and Maidstone. The address of the head office is:

National Schizophrenia Fellowship
28 Castle Street
Kingston-upon-Thames
Surrey KT1 1SS
0208 547 3937

SANE

SANE stands for Schizophrenia — A National Emergency. The organization was established in 1986, following a campaign by Marjorie Wallace in *The Times* on 'the forgotten illness'. SANE has three main aims:

- to increase awareness of the problems of people with schizophrenia
- to provide information and support to sufferers and carers
- to conduct research

Awareness is increased by public awareness campaigns in the media, and by lobbying MPs. Information and support is provided by the 'SANELINE' service. SANELINE is a telephone crisis line that takes calls every day of the year between the hours of 2 pm and 12 midnight. It is manned by volunteers who have been trained to listen to people's problems and give advice, counselling, and information on sources of help.

> ■ The telephone number for SANELINE is 0345 678 000 (local call rates charged)

As well as the crisis line, SANE funds the Sturt Enterprise for Sheltered Employment, a legal information service, and the publication of regular newsletters. SANE funds research into the causes of mental illness, and has already allocated more than £400,000 to research grants.

VOICES

Voices is a service jointly funded by the NSF and SANE. It aims to advise and support sufferers of schizophrenia.

THE SAMARITANS

The Samaritans offer confidential telephone counselling to anyone passing through a difficult period, a personal crisis, and at risk of taking their own lives. The telephone number is 01753 532 713.

Conclusion

■ If you are caring for someone with schizophrenia and finding it hard going, maybe even feeling desperate and suicidal yourself, please don't despair, give someone a ring now. Your own family doctor, CPN, or social worker will be more than happy to help you. Alternatively, if you don't feel comfortable speaking to one of them, ring one of the voluntary organizations listed in this Chapter now.

Much can be done to make your task easier and you are not alone!

Appendix: some commonly used words and phrases explained

AKATHISIA – a distressing side effect of drug treatment, which is a sensation of inner and muscular tension and can be mistaken for the agitation of acute illness with restlessness, pacing, and repeated sitting and standing.

ANTIPSYCHOTIC DRUGS – drugs which control symptoms of schizophrenia, usually long-term, and other serious mental illnesses. (Also known as major tranquillisers and neuroleptic drugs.)

ANXIETY MANAGEMENT – psychological techniques based on 'talking and doing' methods aimed at helping people control anxiety symptoms using eg, deep breathing, relaxation exercises, distraction, and graded exposure to feared situations.

CARE AT HOME – people who are not too ill can be treated at home and visit hospital as outpatients.

CARE IN THE COMMUNITY – local health and social services assess what a person's needs are and give help that takes account of religious, cultural or language needs.

CARE PLAN – a plan which addresses a person's social, medical and nursing needs — it is drawn up as part of the Care Programme Approach CPA).

CARE PROGRAMME APPROACH (CPA) – professionals from health services and the local authority arrange care together. The CPA applies to all patients accepted for care by the specialist mental health services.

CHRONIC/ACUTE/SUB-ACUTE – these terms refer to lengths of illness, although the term 'acute' can also mean severe.

CLINICAL PSYCHOLOGISTS – encourage patients to talk about feelings and worries and help to work out a plan of action so patients can understand the reasons for problems and do something positive about them.

COGNITIVE THERAPY – (also called cognitive–behavioural therapy) is a short-term 'talking and doing' treatment that uses collaboration between therapist and patient to alter unwanted patterns of thinking and behaving. The techniques used include identifying and studying unwanted thought processes, scheduling activities using diaries, increasing a sense of mastery and pleasure from activities, tackling tasks and problems in a graded fashion, and rehearsing new patterns of thinking and behaviour.

COMMISSION FOR RACIAL EQUALITY – helps individuals with cases of racial discrimination, investigates incidences of discrimination and works to promote good race relations. The telephone number is 0171 828 7022.

COMMUNITY MENTAL HEALTH CENTRE – a local base in the community where patients meet members of the mental health team.

COMMUNITY MENTAL HEALTH NURSES – have experience of working in hospitals as well as in the community and can administer medication or injections, provide 'talking' treatments and long-term support. They were previously known as community psychiatric nurses.

COMMUNITY MENTAL HEALTH TEAM (CMHT) – a group of mental health professionals, (eg, doctors, nurses, psychologists, social workers, occupational therapists, therapists and support nurses) based in the community and responsible for caring for, helping and treating patients in the community.

DAY CENTRES – give continued support and help people prepare for everyday life.

DAY HOSPITALS – a person can be admitted to day hospital to receive treatment and support but still return home at the end of each day.

DELUSION – a false belief out of keeping with reality and with the shared beliefs of the person's background and culture.

DELUSION OF GRANDEUR – the patient's belief that they are self-important, great, or superior. (The patient may believe he or she can do anything: break sports records at will, influence people by telepathy, have fabulous wealth, etc.)

DELUSION OF PERSECUTION – the patient believes they are being victimized by one or more individuals or groups, (eg, the IRA, CIA or Masonic Lodges).

DEPOT INJECTIONS – deep muscle injections containing drugs that are slowly released into the body — particularly useful for patients who often forget or are reluctant to take their tablet medication regularly.

DROP-IN CENTRES – give people a chance to meet others with similar problems.

ECT (ELECTRO-CONVULSIVE THERAPY) – sounds dramatic but is a safe hospital treatment which can help people to recover quickly. It is seldom used for people with schizophrenia, except when they are either in a stupor or in a state of great agitation and excitement and dangerously ill through exhaustion and not eating or drinking — or when they have severe depressive illness.

EXPRESSED EMOTION (also known as EE) – includes critical remarks and hostility towards the sufferer, but also expressions of emotional over-involvement, over-protectiveness, and 'smothering'.

EXTRAPYRAMIDAL SIDE-EFFECTS – stiffness and trembling, as seen in Parkinson's disease. These occur in about one-third of patients on traditional antipsychotic medication and can be treated with anti-parkinsonian drugs.

GENERAL PRACTITIONER (GP) – the main person responsible for caring and day-to-day treatment, usually involved in crises and in referral to specialist treatment.

GROUP HOMES/FLATLETS – offer a chance to people discharged from hospital to live with friends, or people they met in hospital.

GROUP/FAMILY THERAPY – these therapies are aimed at the group or family unit rather than the individual patient. The unit is seen as not working properly and techniques are aimed at helping the group or family to function better as a whole. No one is blamed, but all are able to contribute to find solutions to improve communication and behaviour patterns.

HALLUCINATION – a sensation or perception when there is nothing there to account for it, for example hearing voices or seeing visions.

HEALTH INFORMATION SERVICE – a national network designed to help callers make better use of NHS services. It is a confidential information service and gives personal counselling and will provide details of sources of help. The telephone number is 0800 665 544.

KEYWORKER – a health or mental health worker appointed to act as the link between patients and other mental health workers to coordinate a person's care package. They will talk to patients, carers and all those involved to make sure that the care plan is working out.

MENTAL HEALTH ACT (1983) – an Act of Parliment which is divided into a number of 'sections' to cover various different situations. The act ensures that mentally ill people get the necessary treatment to ease their problems, even when they can't see the need for treament themselves. Chapter 6 gives further details.

MENTAL HEALTH ACT COMMISSION – is a special health authority which consists of lawyers, doctors, nurses and lay people — their main function is to review use of the Mental Health Act. They investigate complaints and are legally entitled to interview patients in hospitals and mental nursing homes. The telephone number is 0115 943 7100.

MIND – is a national organization working for a better life for people diagnosed as having mental illness. The telephone number is 0345 660 163 (local call rates charged) or 0208 522 1728 in London.

NATIONAL SCHIZOPHRENIA FELLOWSHIP – is a national organization which provides information and services for those suffering from schizophrenia and their relatives, friends and carers. The telephone number is 0208 547 3937.

NEGATIVE SYMPTOMS (OF SCHIZOPHRENIA) – these include blunted emotions, lack of interest and energy, apathy and social withdrawal.

NEUROLEPTIC DRUGS – drugs which control symptoms of schizophrenia and other, usually long-term, mental illness (also known as major tranquillisers and antipsychotic drugs).

NON-COMPLIANCE (also known as NON-ADHERENCE and, sometimes, NON-CONCORDANCE) – failure to follow an agreed treatment plan, such as taking medication.

NURSING HOMES – provide patients with support and care in a homely environment.

OCCUPATIONAL THERAPISTS – professionals trained to help patients develop confidence and practical skills for living independently, eg, shopping or cooking. They use creative activities, eg, dance and music, to help to release tension and increase self-expression.

POSITIVE SYMPTOMS – these include hallucinations, delusions, disturbed thought processes which show themselves as incoherent speech, illogical thinking, etc, and bizarre patterns of behaviour.

PSYCHIATRISTS – medically trained doctors specially trained to diagnose mental and physical illness and to prescribe the appropriate treatment. They usually work closely with other professionals in community mental health teams.

RELAPSE – this is a return of symptoms of illness occurring during a period of remission from illness (see below).

REMISSION – a relatively brief period during which a person who has been ill has no symptoms.

RESIDENTIAL CARE HOMES – provide people with a supportive environment and trained staff to look after them.

RESPITE CARE/CRISIS UNIT – patients can be admitted to an acute psychiatric unit for a short stay if they are particularly unwell, or to give relatives and carers a break during a crisis.

THE SAMARITANS – this organization offers confidential telephone counselling to anyone passing through a difficult period, a personal crisis, and at risk of taking their own lives. The telephone number is 01753 532 713.

SANE – this organization provides care, awareness and research in schizophrenia and other mental health illnesses. It has a comprehensive database of organizations and self-help groups and can refer enquirers to local services. SANELINE operates a helpline for 365 days of the year; the telephone number is 0345 678 000.

SOCIAL WORKERS – can assess people's needs in the community and try to ensure that these are met. They provide people with care and help to deal with the problems of everyday living as well as problems within families. Specialist mental health social workers are called Approved Social Workers.

SUPERVISION REGISTER – an official list of all patients who, according to all concerned, are at significant risk of suicide, self-neglect or injury, or of seriously harming other people. Only a consultant psychiatrist may place a patient's name on the Supervision Register. The point is to help local health and social services make sure that particularly vulnerable or needy patients are given the care they need and to keep a close check on their progress.

VOLUNTARY GROUPS – work alongside local services to provide care and support for people with mental illness.